THE WORLD'S STRANGEST
AIRCRAFT

THE WORLD'S STRANGEST
AIRCRAFT

Michael Taylor

MetroBooks

EXPERIMENTAL

This edition published by MetroBooks, an imprint of Friedman/Fairfax Publishers, by arrangement with Regency House Publishing Ltd

2001 MetroBooks

M 10 9 8 7 6 5 4 3 2 1

ISBN 1-58663-212-4

5th printing

Regency House Publishing Ltd
3 Mill Lane,
Broxbourne
Hertfordshire
EN10 7AZ
United Kingdom

Printed in Hong Kong
By Sino Publishing House Limited.

All photographs in this book are supplied by the author.

FRONT COVER: Westland P12 tandem-wing beach-straffing aircraft.
BACK COVER: The first Northrop YB-49, with other YB35s under conversion in the backgound to YB-49 and YRB-49 configuration.
BACK COVER INSETS: Top left: Artist's drawing of a Hiller VZ-1 Do-Nut one-man infantry VTOL flying platform of 1959, of which two were built for experimental trials with the US Army. It used a ducted propeller to provide thrust.
Below right: A Lockheed XFV-1 Salmon tail-sitting fighter from the US Naval Avaition Museum. Austin Brown.
PAGES 2-3: Farner HF Colibri 1 SL powered sailplane.
Martin Fricke
THESE PAGES: Lockheed XFV-1 Salmon in horizontal flight, with temporary horizontal undercarriage attached for early flight trials.

Contents

Introduction

This book is dedicated to those flying machines of all periods of aviation history that were somewhat less than conventional in configuration or purpose. Of course, what constitutes 'strange' is subjective, and I make no apologies for my selection or for aircraft that have been omitted because of lack of space.

Many of the most important milestones in aviation development have been attained by unconventional aircraft, and perhaps the majority of pioneering 'stick and string' aeroplanes built at the very dawn of heavier-than-air flying fit into this category. But certain guidelines have to be observed, viewed from the privileged position of hindsight. Often a good place to start when looking for 'strange' types is among records of those that are least remembered because of the small number built. Of course, it always has to be realized that any particular flying machine from the past might look bizarre to us in retrospect, yet could have been viewed as a perfectly sensible line of approach to contemporary onlookers. Similarly, strange-looking aircraft that we know flew well and so tend to view in a different light, might have been seen as 'barking mad' at the time. So often are our conceptions coloured by achievement, and maybe this is correct.

It would be a mistake, however, to assume that all unusual-looking aircraft were eventually assigned to the dustbin of history, especially those built as one-offs or in tiny numbers for research alone. This could not be further from the truth. Amongst 'strange' aircraft that proved to be highly successful in their assigned tasks and helped take aviation knowledge to new levels of excellence can be counted the Bell X-1, the first aircraft to 'break the sound barrier'. This little rocket-powered aeroplane, air-dropped from a bomber, was intended only for research and had no production counterpart whatsoever. Yet, so great was its achievement that it carved a place in the history of the world and the endeavours of man. Moreover, some of the strangest aircraft flying today are full production types, including the Lockheed Martin F-117 pyramidal stealth fighter and Northrop Grumman B-2 flying-wing stealth bomber, both operational with the USAF.

In this book, I have striven to detail the strange aircraft within the context of the wider aspect. This helps comparison between the accepted 'norm' of the time and the more unusual machines described here. This is particularly important for the earliest periods, when what was 'conventional' had still to be established.

MJHT, March 1996

The Minerva, *a fanciful aerial exploration balloon engraved at the Ordnance Survey Office in England in 1864, having been conceived by Professor Robertson as a floating garrison with detachable small balloon, steerable parachute, cannon armament and much more.*

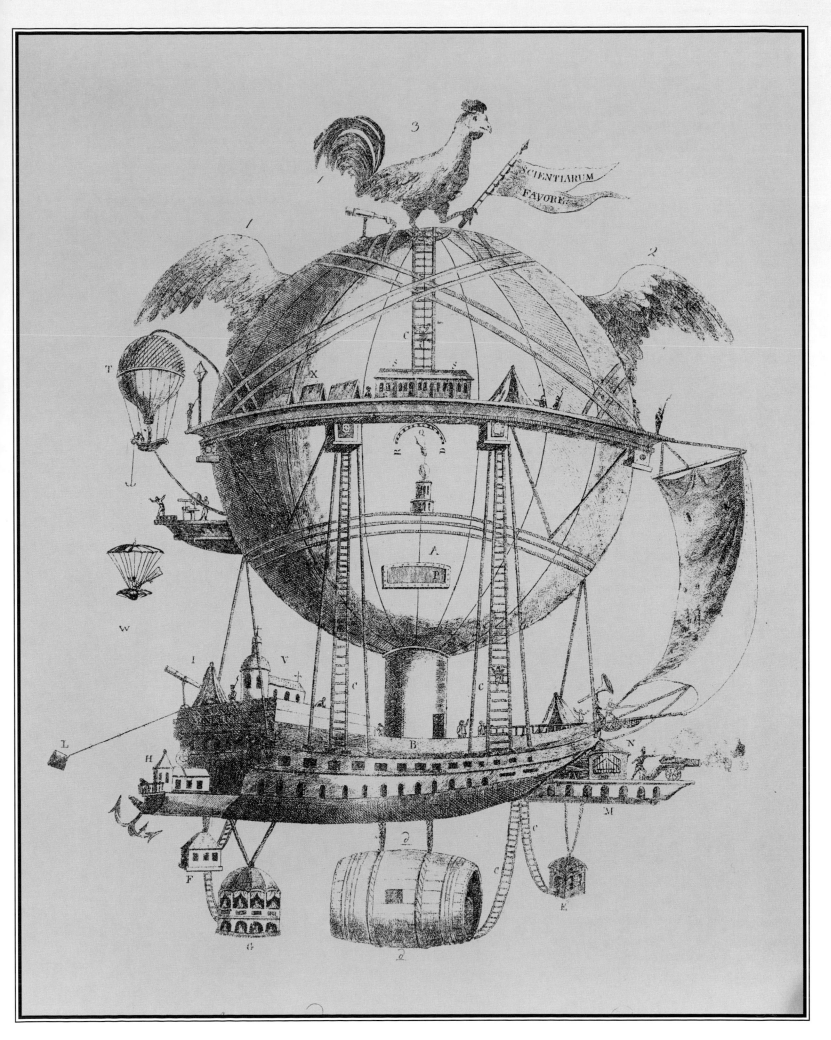

Chapter One
Experiments and Adventures in the Atmosphere

'There are epochs in the history of every great operation and in the course of every undertaking, to which the co-operation of successive generations of men have contributed..., when it becomes desirable to pause for a while, and, as it were, to take stock; to review the progress made, and estimate the amount of work done: not so much for complacency, as for the purpose of forming a judgement of the efficiency of the methods resorted to, to do it; as to lead us to inquire how they may yet be improved, if such improvement be possible, to accelerate the furtherance of the object, or to ensure the ultimate perfection of its attainments. In scientific, no less than in material and social undertaking, such pauses and *résumés* are eminently useful, and are sometimes forced on our considerations by a conjuncture of circumstances which almost of necessity obliges us to take a *coup d'œil* of the whole subject, and make up our minds, not only as to validity of what is done, but of the manner in which it has been done, the methods employed, and the direction in which we are henceforth to proceed, and probability of further progress.'
Sir John Frederck William Herschel (1792-1871)

Herschel's words, included in the remarkable *Astra Castra - Experiments and Adventures in the Atmosphere*, a book published in 1865, appeared in print just a few years before the very first 'hop' flights of any sort were achieved by powered and piloted aeroplanes, though several decades before the Wright brothers truly advanced flying theory into fact. Herschel had witnessed in his lifetime the routine use of free-flying balloons and the creation of steerable airships, but a greater challenge lay ahead and only through a complete rethink of the science of flying would aviation be able to move on to new heights. It was, as Herschel predicted, necessary to stand back from the accepted means of flight before progressing along a new and difficult path that could (and did) lead to even greater successes, this time with powered aeroplanes.

Yet, by the very nature of the earliest experiments to devise suitable heavier-than-air aircraft capable of sustaining a pilot in powered flight, when the greatest inspiration came from examining birds and bats, many of the first aeroplanes were 'strange' to our modern thinking. Sir George Cayley had, by the 1850s, demonstrated at Scarborough in England on more than one occasion that fixed-wing gliders could be built capable of carrying a person, but powered ascending flight was a more difficult proposition and required a less simple approach.

Two principal lines of thinking developed for powered flight. One was to experiment with flapping or oscillating wings, in an attempt to mechanically reproduce nature. Such machines are collectively known as ornithopters and many varied types were constructed. However, whilst some scale models could be made to fly, the concept for larger piloted machines was scientifically flawed. Among the best-known series of experiments with ornithopters were those conducted in Britain by E. P Frost, carried out over a period of more than a decade during the late 19th and early 20th centuries. Frost tried both steam and, for the 1903 ornithopter, a 3 hp BAT petrol internal combustion engine to provide the power for wing flapping, but none of his machines could lift the pilot from the ground. Frost's machines were, though, lovingly constructed of canes, silk and thousands of actual bird feathers, and examples are preserved in museums today.

It is interesting to note that Frost had clearly expected the use of bird feathers to contribute in some measure to successful flight. In this he reasserted a myth that can be traced back to at least the early 16th century, at which time John Damian, then Abbot of Tungland in Galloway, Scotland, tried to fly from the walls of Stirling Castle to France. Not surprisingly, he crashed to the ground and was lucky that he broke only a thigh bone. Left unrepentant by his miscalculation, he blamed the misfortune on his having used some feathers from dunghill fowls (ground birds) instead of using only those from high-flying eagles.

Yet, Frost was not to be the last to construct ornithopters by a long way. Even after fixed-wing aeroplanes were flying highly successfully on both sides of the Atlantic, there were those in various countries who would not let go of the concept. In 1910, the year after Blériot had flown the English Channel and the world distance record for fixed-wing aeroplanes stood at about 300 miles (500 km), a Monsieur Passat began constructing an ornithopter with four wings, the rear pair being made to flap using a 4.5 hp motorcycle engine. One of Passat's few concessions to 'modern science', apart from the internal combusion engine and welded steel tube structure with fabric covering, was the absence of feathers, though the whole machine remained very 'bird-like' in design. During trials on Wimbledon Common, England in 1912, Passat's ornithopter actually managed to leave the ground at a speed of under 15 miles per hour (24 km/h), flapping its way into the air for a 'hop' of 400 feet (122 m), before meeting a tree. Far from deterred, he continued his experiments with improved machines over the coming years and in the face of growing redicule, as did other

E. P. Frost with one of his ornithopters after the turn of the century.
Philip Jarrett collection.

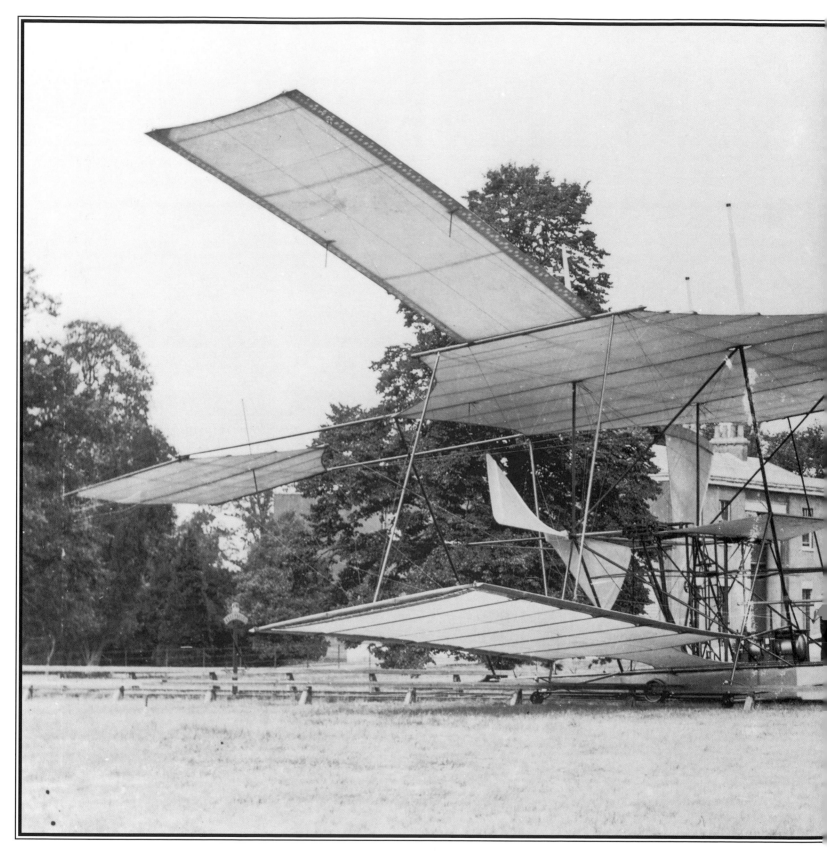

inventors in the blind faith that the birds had to be right!

The second line of thinking was to adopt fixed wings, with the engine driving one or more propellers to produce aerodynamic thrust. Among the many problems that had to be overcome by early would-be aviators was the lack of any suitably light yet powerful engine for full-sized craft. Though both large and small steam engines were available in the 19th century, their weight-to-power ratio was restrictive. One possible solution, as adopted by Sir Hiram Maxim (inventor of the Maxim machine-gun) for his test rig flying machine, was to select extremely powerful steam engines and match them to an outsized airframe with outrageously large wings. The octagonal main centre-section, together with lateral and other surfaces, totalled 4,000 square feet (371.6 m²), and the rig used two 180 hp compound engines supplied with steam via a remarkable marine boiler incorporating a

damaged during this trial, it was repaired. The next stage was to attempt actual flight. For this, a special 'railway track' was laid along which to gather speed, with superimposed guard rails of Georgia pine above to restrict flight to two feet (0.6 m). On 31 July that year, after a run of 600 feet (183 m) and a speed approaching 40 miles per hour (64 km/h), the machine lifted with such force that it broke a guard rail. Power was thrown and it came down off the track, sustaining damage. Here the trials ended for good. Total distance from start to finish of the run was some 1,000 feet (305 m). Although many thousands of pounds had been spent, the 'flight' marked the end of Maxim's aeroplane experiments until 1910, when he produced a more conventional three-seat biplane which did not progress beyond tethered testing. Although this man of great renown in many spheres contributed little to the progress of flying, he was among a very select few actually to fly steam-powered aeroplanes.

History recalls that the very first piloted

gas-burner with 7,650 jets, driving two 17-foot 10-inch (5.44-m) propellers.

In 1894, after three years of construction, Maxim's machine was ready for trials. Concerned that it should not take-off uncontrollably, he first tested it at Baldwyn's Park in Kent, England, with very heavy wheels to prevent lift off. Although

LEFT
Maxim biplane at Baldwyn's Park.
Philip Jarrett collection.

ABOVE
Ader's Avion III *military aeroplane, displayed at the Musée de l'Air, Paris.*
Austin J. Brown.

aeroplane to fly from level ground was the *Éole*, on 9 October 1890 at the Château of Madame Pereire, Armainvilliers. The invention of Frenchman Clément Ader, it was a staging post between old and new thinking, with strange but non-flapping bat-like wings of hollow ribs and silk, and a primitive tractor propeller powered by a 20 hp steam engine. While it is true that the flight on the 9th had been unsustainable, covering only 165 feet (50 m) and barely clearing the ground, and that the aircraft was virtually uncontrollable, it gave rise to much optimism. Sadly, Ader's attempts to build upon this start were unsuccessful, his *Avion III*, built to a French Ministry of War contract as a two-seater with a 165-pound (75-kg) bomb load, only partly lifting from its circular test track at Satorg in 1897.

As with others before him, Ader too had at first looked at bird feathers as a possible key to achieving lift, and in 1873 had constructed a large man-carrying 'bird' with goose feathers for captive lift experiments against strong wind. These experiments convinced Ader that non-flapping curved wings were the answer to flight, though his subsequent *Éole* would owe more to bats than birds in appearance, with featherless wings that could be warped and the curvative altered to theoretically provide control and lift (and could be folded away).

During the final decade of the 19th century, if anyone appeared likely to produce a powered aeroplane capable of sustained flight, that person was odds-on to be the German Otto Lilienthal. Between 1891 and 1896, Lilienthal had built and flown (over two thousand flights) a series of extremely successful monoplane and biplane fixed-wing hang gliders, on occasions flying more than 800 feet (250 m) distance and sometimes rising above his starting height. Tragically, he died on 10 August 1896 following a crash the previous day, having already begun work on a powered version of a glider. Though none of his gliders can be termed 'strange' in the context of this book – indeed they were the most elegant and far-sighted aircraft to date

– Lilienthal had strangely resisted the lure of propellers in favour of flapping wingtip paddles for his powered machine, to be driven by a carbonic acid gas motor.

Power for Progress

If there was one single device that proved to be the catalyst that sparked the reinvention of the aeroplane into a worthwhile machine, it was the internal combustion engine. In 1877, Nikolaus Otto had conceived the four-

stroke petrol internal combustion engine. A practical single-cylinder example was the creation of Gottlieb Daimler of the Otto factory in 1884, which in the following year was used to drive a Benz motorcycle. The internal combustion engine was also ideal for aviation, and an early application took place in 1888, when Dr Wölfert of Germany flew a balloon which had a 2 hp Daimler petrol engine installed.

If developed to produce greater output, the same type of engine could knock spots off steam for aeroplanes, and this was quickly realized by the most innovative designers. The honour of being first to produce such a marriage of petrol engine and airframe for a piloted aeroplane went to Austrian William Kress, who in 1893 (at the age of 57) had begun an engineering course at the Vienna polytechnic. Five years later

he started work on an aeroplane intended to operate from water and snow. The three sets of tandem wings had wooden ribs, but the remainder of the airframe used a structure of steel tubing, all mounted on two aluminium floats with snow rails. In this very advanced structure he wanted to install a 40 hp engine weighing 441 pounds (200 kg), but no supplier seemed capable of matching the required output to weight.

Replica of Alberto Santos-Dumont's unusual tail-first biplane, the 14-bis , belonging to the Aeroclube de São Paulo. Austin J. Brown.

However, in 1901 Mercedes delivered a 30 hp engine (Daimler type), though weighing 838 pounds (380 kg). That October the seaplane, now substantially overweight, unstable and floating low in the water at Tullnerbach reservoir, nevertheless gathered good speed with Kress on board and the floats slowly started to rise from the water. Unfortunately, a stone groyne loomed close and Kress had to shut down the engine and attempt to manoeuvre past. Already unstable, the wind caught the underside of the wings and the machine flipped over, breaking up. Clinging to a float, Kress was pulled from the reservoir twenty minutes later. The seaplane was partially mended in 1902, but was never completely rebuilt.

Over the next two years, various piloted aeroplanes with petrol engines achieved 'hop' flights, including those by Richard Pearse in far-away New Zealand and Carl Jatho in Germany. In the USA, Samuel Pierpont Langley constructed the first aeroplane to make a sustained flight on the power of a petrol engine, though this was a quarter-scale unmanned model intended only as a stepping stone towards a full-scale version. It is a matter of historical record that Langley's full-size *Aerodrome* was unsuccessfully launched from a houseboat on the Potomac River in October and again in December 1903, just before the Wright brothers achieved their historic first-ever piloted, powered and controlled flight on 17 December that year.

Years of careful research, including wind tunnel testing and manned glider flying, had brought success to Orville and Wilbur Wright. Indeed, such was their lead that on 5 October 1905 Wilbur piloted the improved *Flyer III* on a flight lasting 38 minutes, of over 24 miles (39 km). Then, incredibly, on the 16th of that month the brothers decided to stop flying (a self-imposed moratorium lasting nearly three years), intending instead to exploit their invention. It was not until 12 November 1906 that a sustained flight was achieved by any another pilot, and even then the Brazilian Alberto Santos-Dumont managed

only 722 feet (220 m) in his unusual tail-first biplane *14-bis* at Bagatelle in France. This tiny distance, however, represented the world's first officially recognized sustained flight and the first ever world distance record for powered aeroplanes, having been witnessed by the Fédération Aéronautique Internationale (FAI) that had been formed in the previous year (the Wright brothers' flights could not be recognized by the FAI).

After the Wrights, no other American successfully flew until 20 June 1908, when Glenn Curtiss piloted the *June Bug* over a distance of 1,266 feet (386 m). On 4 July he covered 5,090 feet (1,551 m) in the biplane, winning the Scientific American trophy for the first official flight in public in the USA of over one kilometre. *June Bug* had been a creation of the Aerial Experiment Association founded by Alexander Graham Bell (inventor of the telephone), and had followed *Red Wing* and *White Wing* which had managed short distances earlier the same year. Other machines were also built and tested by the Association, including one of extraordinary configuration. *Cygnet II* was the creation of Bell and another Association member and pilot, J.A.D. McCurdy. Comprising 5,500 tetrahedral cells, it followed the *Cygnet I* unpowered 'aerodrome kite' that had been towed by a motorboat for two flights in December 1907. Pilot on *Cygnet I* had been Lt Thomas Selfridge, who fortunately escaped unhurt from the accident on the second trial that wrecked the aircraft. The powered *Cygnet II* itself was tested over the frozen lake at Baddeck Bay, Nova Scotia, on 22 February 1909 but failed to fly. The next day, another of the Association's aeroplanes, the *Silver Dart*, was flown by McCurdy at Baddeck Bay to record the first aeroplane flight of any sort in Canada and the first powered and sustained aeroplane flight in the British Empire, covering over 4 miles (6.5 km).

Tragically, by then Lt Thomas Selfridge had been killed (on 17 September 1908) while the passenger on a Wright biplane flown by Orville during military trials for

ABOVE
Aerial Experiment Association Cygnet II *at Baddeck Bay, Nova Scotia.*
Via Philip Jarrett/National Museum of Science & Technology.

RIGHT
Phillips 1907 Multiplane.
Philip Jarrett collection.

the US Army, the first fatality of a powered aeroplane accident.

The first powered and manned aeroplane flight in Britain (not sustained: see also McCurdy, p.14) is generally attributed to Horatio Phillips, with a machine built a little earlier than the *Cygnet II* and almost as strange. The 1907 *Multiplane* used four banks of wings, each bank comprising 50 individual and superimposed very narrow-chord surfaces. Power came from a 22 hp engine. In mid-1907, at Streatham in south London, it took off at 30 miles per hour (48 km/h) on a stable though short flight of approximately 500 feet (152 m). This was the crowning achievement for Phillips, whose earlier steam-powered *Multiplane* of 1893 had flown a short distance at Harrow but only with a 72-pound (33-kg) weight representing a pilot, and his manned 1904 *Multiplane* with one bank of twenty superimposed wings and a 22 hp engine had proved unstable and incapable of its task.

Many individual wings (some with anhedral or dihedral) were also built into the oval structure of the flying machine associated with the Marquis of D'Equevillery, which was expected to take-off on the power of a mere 7 or 8 hp engine. Not altogether surprisingly, there is no record of it ever flying.

And so towards War

Despite some amusing hiccups, by 1908 the main parameters for good flying machines had been established, though aeroplanes took many individual forms as no single type entered production until the following year, when Short Brothers signed an agreement with Wilbur Wright for the series-production of six Wright biplanes at Leysdown in England. To encourage even greater efforts, large money prizes were by

Marquis D'Equevillery's multiplane.
Philip Jarrett collection.

then being offered for significant flying achievements. Such was the growing competence of the machines being built in various interested countries that it was decided to hold the first-ever International Aviation Meeting. This took place at Reims in France in August 1909, and twenty-three of the thirty-eight aeroplanes entered actually flew. This ensured even greater public interest and led to worldwide publicity.

1909 was, of course, the year Louis Blériot flew the English Channel (19 July), winning a £1,000 prize offered by the Daily Mail newspaper; ominously, it was also the year the US Army bought a Wright Model A as the world's first military aeroplane for service, costing the government a total of $30,000! It also marked the eclipse of the Wright brothers' dominance over all comers, although on the final day of 1908 Wilbur Wright had set a world distance record of 77.48 miles (124.7 km) at Auvours in France. It had taken a very long time for the rest of the world to catch up, helped by the years the brothers had stopped flying, but now the Wrights would never again enjoy a lead. By August 1909, Henry Farman had flown his biplane over 111 miles (180 km), and on 13 October 1913 an improved Farman biplane, flown by A. Seguin, set the final world distance record before the First World War, at an amazing 634 miles (1,021 km).

There is little doubt that France had by then become *the* aviation nation in the world, and French machines formed the backbone of several combatant nations after war broke out. Yet, despite impressive feats by 'conventional' aeroplanes, there remained as always those willing to put their own ideas to the test. Just occasionally, such ideas were successful.

In Britain Cedric Lee, who had bought the patented rights to annular wings, and G. Tilghman Richards produced an annular wing biplane in 1911, which had not proved satisfactory and was, anyway, destroyed inside its hangar during a storm that winter. A glider with a semi-circular upper wing and full annular lower wing followed and

Lee and Richards annular monoplane.
Philip Jarrett collection.

was flown in 1912. Wind tunnel tests also confirmed that the annular wing concept was perfectly sound, with the added advantage that there appeared to be no *burble point* at which angle-of-attack the wing would otherwise sustain an abrupt disruption to the unseparated flow. Moreover, the wingspan could be considerably less than for other aircraft while maintaining adequate area, and stall was docile.

Armed with such results, a new two-seat monoplane was constructed with a 22-foot (6.7-m) annular wing. Powered by an excellent 80 hp Gnome engine, this monoplane was first flown on 23 November 1913 but with terrible consequences. Having taken off rapidly, the machine proved tail heavy. Then suddenly it stalled, a tragic accident being avoided only by the intervention of fortunately placed telegraph wires which broke the fall. Repaired twice after accidents, and modified, it

subsequently became very airworthy and accumulated a large number of flights right up to the outbreak of war. Construction of further examples was started in 1914 but the design concept failed to gain general acceptance.

Interestingly, a much larger and more primitive rhomboidal-winged biplane had appeared in Britain in 1911 as the Edwards *Rhomboidal*, the 50 hp Humber engine driving two large propellers turning within the mainplanes. This is not thought to have flown during trials at Brooklands.

One of the most striking occurrences of pre-First World War flying came with the incredible exploits of the French Deperdussin 'monocoque' monoplane racer, built to compete in the Gordon-Bennet Cup held at Reims in 1913. Far from being strange in configuration, it was a masterpiece of design and engineering, and so advanced for its time that it is hard to place it as a pre-war machine. On 29

18

September that year it became the first-ever aircraft to fly at over 200 km/h, recording 126.666 miles per hour (205.85 km/h) in the hands of Frenchman Maurice Prévost. Using a 160 hp Gnome engine to drive a propeller with large spinner, and with inversely tapering wings (trailing edge) cropped for record-breaking, it smashed twelve world records. However, though of aerodynamically clean design and faster than almost any coming wartime fighter, it does not seem to have influenced planners to any great degree and, indeed, was viewed by some almost as a freak with absolutely no possible practical use whatsoever beyond the attainment of speed. Wartime Deperdussins and related SPADS were, therefore, significantly less advanced in many important respects, though maybe far more 'practical'.

Britain, too, produced a pre-war masterpiece, as the Royal Aircraft Factory Scouting Experimental 4, or S.E.4. As with the Deperdussin, it had a monocoque fuselage, similar Gnome engine and a propeller spinner, but was a braced biplane. An incredible initiative for the time was the adoption of a moulded celluloid cockpit canopy, though this was removed when pilots refused to be enclosed.

During trials in 1914, the S.E.4 attained 135 miles per hour (217 km/h), an extraordinary feat that was never officially recorded as a world record. However, the engine proved unreliable and was replaced by a 100 hp Monosoupape Gnome. So powered, the aircraft's speed fell by over 40 miles per hour (64 km/h). No production of the S.E.4 followed, though it was still one of the fastest aircraft in the world.

Great War Gambles

In October 1914 a prototype fighter designed by a Russian Army officer, Aleksandr Bezobrazov, flew for the first time, only weeks after Germany and Russia went to war. It was one of the strangest aircraft to be tested by any nation, with slender triplane wings mounted at such an acute stagger that the lowest planes were only just ahead of the vertical tail, while the upper planes projected massively forward of the front of the fuselage. Not altogether surprisingly, it was not adopted for service.

Despite this bold concept and other attempts by designers in combatant nations to try out new airframe arrangements, the vast majority of aircraft produced during the First World War remained 'conventional'. Progress in general operating capability, therefore, came mainly from the availability of much more powerful and reliable aero-engines, arguably the single most vital development of the entire war. It is true that pre-war attempts to arm aircraft were brought to fruition during this conflict, and nobody should overlook the significance of the propeller-synchronized forward-firing machine-gun, but with greater engine power

came more speed, more altitude, faster climb, more warload and greater airframe weights, all necessary to the war effort and the growing sophistication of uses for aeroplanes.

Also in Russia, though back in May 1913, Igor Sikorsky had been responsible for the world's first four-engined aircraft to fly, the *Le Grand*, from which the world's first four-engined bombers to see active service were derived as Ilya Mourometz biplanes. Unfortunately, these bombers suffered greatly from a shortage of suitable engines, often having to make do with other types than the preferred Samson-built Canton-Unnés. Even with Canton-Unnés, for a bomber with a wingspan in Type B form of over 101 feet (31 m) and weighing 10,600 pounds (4,800 kg), a total output from all four engines of 670 hp was hardly adequate and provided a speed of only 60 miles per hour (96 km/h).

As the war progressed, more powerful engines were produced on both sides of the trenches. Fighters gained important speed and climb advantages from inline engines often of 200 hp or more, or from considerably less-powerful but highly-

developed rotary engines such as the 130 hp Clerget on the Sopwith Camel. But it was the bombers that really made use of extra horsepower. The single 375 hp Rolls-Royce Eagle engine adopted for the British D.H.4 light bomber of 1917 provided adequate output to permit a 460-pound (208-kg) bombload, while a speed of 143 miles per hour (230 km/h) meant it was faster than the fighters. The follow-on D.H.9A of 1918 went a stage further and had a 400 hp American Liberty 12 engine installed, a hugely powerful engine for the time, this heavier aircraft losing a little speed in comparison with the D.H.4 but gaining an extra 200 pounds (91 kg) of bombs. For heavy bombing, the RAF's 100-foot (30.5-m) wingspan Handley Page O/400 of 1918 had two 360 hp Eagles, giving a speed of 97 miles per hour (156 km/h) and permitting a 2,000-pound (907-kg) bombload.

Italy and others also tailored better aeroplanes to the latest engines, and Italian Caproni multi-engined bombers are particularly remembered. Yet no nation worked so hard as Germany to perfect the giant bomber, principally because of the failure of its rigid airships to bomb the

Allies out of the war. Records indicate that the largest operational aeroplane of the war was the Zeppelin-Staaken R VI, at over 138 feet (42.2 m) span, but this giant was given only four 245 hp Maybach or 260 hp Mercedes D IVa engines, allowing a maximum speed of just 84 miles per hour (135 km/h) and a bombload for short distance raids that was no greater than the Handley Page. The fact that Germany failed to develop operational engines of huge output for general use was a major miscalculation, and even the more famous Friedrichshafen and Gotha heavy bombers had to make do with just two Mercedes D IVa engines.

Among giant German bombers destined not to reach front-line service was the Linke-Hofmann R I, of which only two prototypes were ever built. Undoubtedly one of the strangest bombers of the war, its ungainly appearance was due almost entirely to wind tunnel research conducted at the Göttingen laboratory that indicated lift-to-drag ratio gains for an aircraft with a fuselage that filled the entire interplane gap between the biplane wings. Interestingly, such theoretical gains were recalculated and

proven post-war, though the concept failed on the R I. In the event, the first R I broke up in mid-air in May 1917, and although the modified second prototype fared better, it eventually flipped over in a landing accident and was abandoned. One major difficulty had been that the pilot sat so high he found it hard to land the aeroplane. The unusual power plant comprised four Mercedes D IVas mounted inside the deep fuselage, driving two large propellers carried between the wings.

When 1919 arrived, it was possible to look back at the aeroplane's performance in its first large-scale war and assess its impact on events. The principal asset had been its usefulness in assisting ground forces through visual and photographic reconnaissance, observation and artillery spotting, and the development of fighters had come about mainly through the need to create suitable conditions in which such reconnaissance types could operate and survive, or indeed the ability to destroy them. True, this had led to fighters on each side patrolling to engage in mutual annihilation, but even this was justified by the need for air supremacy. Perhaps only

the bombers showed what air forces were capable of achieving through their own deeds rather than actions aimed at assisting the armies. These largest of aeroplanes actually caused little carnage during strategic raids but were highly effective in tying up defence forces far out of proportion to the inflicted damage. And, equally importantly, many were eminently convertible into post-war commercial hacks, invaluable in the establishment of pioneering airline services.

Chapter Two
Peace, Problems and Prototypes

The First World War had forced mass industrialization of the aircraft industry, with thousands of aeroplanes and tens of thousands of engines constructed in 1918 alone on huge production lines in vast buildings. On the surface it appeared that the speed, size and capabilities of the latest warplanes were the results of major technical advances, whereas in truth the need to rush new machines to the front lines had meant much greater reliance on better engines for improved performance rather than achievable gains through aerodynamic efficiency. Perhaps with peace, the giant manufacturers would have the time to explore such efficiencies? Initially, the reality was somewhat different.

With the artistice, and huge stockpiles of brand new but now unwanted aeroplanes (many still crated and soon to be offered for sale at rock-bottom prices), the plug was inevitably pulled on the majority of outstanding production orders. The British aircraft industry, in particular, was savaged by abrupt cancellations, and whilst some manufacturers survived the cuts by constructing boats, buses, motorcycles, sheds and other items to supplement limited aircraft building, some famous names just went to the wall. As for the large fighting forces themselves, the Royal Air Force (for example) had by late 1919 been whittled down from 188 operational

squadrons and a total inventory of 22,650 aircraft to just twelve squadrons, with obvious consequences to manufacturers looking for any post-war business.

What little immediate work there was came from small-sized military orders, niche markets or for export, and in consequence considerable emphasis shifted to commercial aviation. The burgeoning airlines, many initially content to operate modified bombers to carry small numbers of passengers or freight and establish air routes, would soon need purpose-designed airliners with which to maximize their business, offering better economies, comfort and passenger numbers. An early short-term solution was to offer brand new airliners based on previous bomber technology, as with the Handley Page W.8 'flying saloon', with seating for fifteen to twenty passengers in an uncluttered cabin or with plenty of room for freight. But such aircraft hardly advanced technology. The German Junkers F 13, on the other hand, appeared more forward-looking with its low-mounted cantilever monoplane wings, and was indeed the world's first purpose-built all-metal airliner to enter service, but this too was little more than a clever adaptation of the wartime J 10 and only carried a crew of two and four passengers (under the terms of the Versailles Treaty, Germany was severely restricted in the type and size of aircraft it was permitted to construct). These, and

many of the aircraft appearing in other countries in the early 1920s, offered little that was truly inspiring.

Enter Caproni

Caproni of Italy had established quite a wartime reputation for its multi-engined bombers. With peace, like many other companies, it quickly set about adapting its designs into giant airliners. A prototype twenty-three passenger triplane with three Liberty engines was joined in 1920 by the prototype of a five-engined monster capable of carrying thirty passengers, each of its three wings having a span of 110 feet (33 m). But these aircraft, though huge, were not particularly inspiring.

Then, in February 1921, taxi trials began on Lake Maggiore of an aircraft that threw caution to the wind. The Caproni Ca 60 Triple Hydro-Triplane was a 100-passenger flying-boat of immense proportions, with three tandem sets of triplane wings and no fewer than eight 400 hp Liberty engines carried in tractor and pusher positions. Yet even this was only intended to be a scale representation of an even larger flying-boat to undertake transatlantic flights, and was to be used to obtain useful data. No conventional elevators were provided, and longitudinal

Caproni Ca 60 Triple Hydro-Triplane.

control was by opposed deflection of the ailerons on the front and aft wings. In the event, longitudinal control proved virtually non-existent.

On 2 March 1921, the Triple Hydro-Triplane made its first flight of about one mile (1.6 km). On 4 March a second flight was attempted. This time, however, the flying-boat began an unplanned descent from which the crew could not recover, despite its best efforts. Inevitably, the aircraft sustained serious hull damage upon alighting and the grand plan was terminated.

Search for Efficiency

While Caproni and others wrestled with their drag-inducing giants, a number of aircraft were appearing that had been designed from the outset to benefit more fully from aerodynamic efficiency, though the results were not always as expected. In the USA, the Remington-Burnelli Aircraft Corporation produced the R.B.1 airliner capable of carrying twenty-five passengers within a fuselage configured as a thick aerofoil section. The two crew occupied open cockpits above the cabin. Drag-inducing engine nacelles were not

necessary, as the twin 420 hp Liberty 12s were installed within the fuselage nose, and only the propellers and radiators spoiled the contours. Thus, the intention was to ensure that the fuselage contributed lift, while its corrugated duralumin skins over a plywood structure added strength. However, although the fuselage was 14 feet (4.3 m) wide, the two 10-foot 3-inch (3.12-m) propellers were so closely positioned that the hubs were just 10 feet 4 inches (3.15 m) apart, reducing the effectiveness of the propellers. Even more importantly, the efficiency of the tail unit and thereby manoeuvrability were impaired to some degree by the fuselage shape.

The R.B.1 was followed in 1924 by the R.B.2, offering certain improvements and a capacious cabin for bulk freight only. Although the position of the propellers remained as before, the engines were 520 hp Galloway Atlantics. Corrugated duralumin now replaced fabric for the wing skins, while the rear of the fuselage tapered to enhance tail control. Still the concept met with no commercial enthusiasm.

Not daunted and now with a new partner, Vincent Burnelli produced the Chapman-Burnelli CB-16 in 1927, a twenty-passenger monoplane with two long fins supporting an entirely new tailplane and elevator arrangement. Power came from two 625 hp Curtiss Conquerors and the mainwheels retracted under the fuselage using a crank system in the cockpit. Maximum speed was an impressive 150 miles per hour (241 km/h). In 1929 a light plane derivative with two 90 hp ADC Cirrus III engines was constructed to take part in the Guggenheim Safe Aircraft competition, as the GX-3, with special features including a variable camber monoplane wing and full-span flaps.

Remington-Burnelli R.B.1 airliner.
Philip Jarrett collection.

About the same time as the GX-3 appeared, a variant of the CB-16 was produced as the UB-20 with stressed metal skins, a fixed undercarriage and 800 hp Packard engines, though with no greater commercial success. Then, in 1934, came the new UB-14. Although based on the same general principles, the fuselage for fourteen passengers was shorter and generally acted as the centre section of the monoplane wings. For the first time the crew had an enclosed cockpit, the twin tail was supported by longer slim booms that performed as extensions to the fin area, and the undercarriage was hydraulically retractable. No attempt was made to enclose the two 680 hp Pratt & Whitney Hornet radial engines within the fuselage, though they remained close set. Unfortunately, in 1935 the UB-14 was lost in a landing accident, and the UB-14B was built as a refined replacement. For a time, it seemed that commercial success might follow, when in 1937 Cunliffe Owen Aircraft was founded in Britain to construct a modified UB-14B as the OA-1, with 710 hp Bristol Perseus engines, but no others followed.

After the Second World War, the Canadian Car & Foundry Company (which held the Canadian licence to Burnelli's patents) formed the Cancargo Aircraft Manufacturing Company to develop and build the CBY-3 Loadmaster, Burnelli's final 'lifting-fuselage' design. The concept had reached maturity and the Loadmaster was an impressive twenty-two passenger transport with a conventional front cockpit and initially fitted with two 1,450 hp Pratt & Whitney Twin-Wasp engines. It still had a flat-sided aerofoil-shaped fuselage but forming booms to the rear for the tail. Yet again, this version failed to spawn production examples, but it became a working transport and as such is a tribute to a designer whose main difficulty had been that he produced aircraft too far ahead of their time.

Others, too, appreciated the benefits of a 'lifting body' fuselage, and in France in the late 1920s Dyle & Bacalan (best known as a naval dockyard) produced the DB 10 night bomber. As with the Burnellis, this strut-braced monoplane had twin engines (480 hp Jupiters) mounted in close proximity, while the two pilots and gunner occupied tandem cockpits in above-fuselage fairings. This remained a prototype. By the early 1930s the aircraft department of Dyle & Bacalan had become Société Aérienne Bordelaise under the management of Nieuport-Delage, taking over the triple-engined DB 70 (first tested in 1929) and DB 71 airliners and developing from them the AB 20 and AB 21 four-engined heavy bombers. All were monoplanes of twin-boom configuration with wingspans of over 120 feet (36 m), each with a fuselage nacelle ahead of the main 'lifting body' fuselage. Accommodation in each airliner comprised two cabins for a total of ten people in the forward section of each boom plus a saloon for eight more at tables in the thick centre-section. The bombers also had glazed leading edges to the thick fuselage section but otherwise were fitted out for offensive operations. Defensive armament for the bombers included a ventral 'dustbin' gun turret. In 1931, the requisitioned DB 70 was used to carry French shock troops during manoeuvres. The DBs and ABs also remained prototypes.

In Germany, Junkers had also been applying itself to the ideal of maximizing lift with passenger accommodation, but the company came up with an entirely different, and in many ways more successful, concept. On 6 November 1929, the 144-foot 4-inch (44-m) wingspan G 38 made its maiden flight. Of all-metal construction with mainly corrugated skins, it appeared to be configured as a fairly typical monoplane until the true size of the wings were taken into account. At such span and chord width, the depth at the roots became sufficient to permit a three-passenger cabin to be

Burnelli UB-14B airliner.
Philip Jarrett collection.

included in the wing leading-edge on each side of the fuselage, with inset glazed panels. Two more passengers occupied the fuselage nose and twenty-six were carried in the conventional fuselage. This giant aircraft was lifted by four engines, eventually of 750 hp each.

Only two G 38s were built, both of them operated commercially by Deutsche Lufthansa. One was lost in 1936 and the other was destroyed during an RAF bombing raid in 1940.

Meanwhile, Mitsubishi of Japan had purchased a licence for the G 38 and went on to produce six modified aircraft between 1931 and 1934 as Ki-20 heavy bombers for the Army, taken into service as Type 92s and expected to have sufficient range to attack the Philippines from bases away from Japan. These, however, were not well received and played no part in any hostilities.

Large though the G 38 undoubtedly was, it was dwarfed by several other landplanes and seaplanes that appeared in the 1930s,

few of which were produced in any quantity. By far the most interesting and probably least remembered was the K-7 built by Kalinin in the Soviet Union. Kalinin produced several designs for aircraft with elliptical wings, and an elliptical monoplane wing of nearly 174 feet (53 m) span was selected for the K-7 that first flew on 11 August 1933. This was almost a 'flying wing', for although it had a conventional cockpit nacelle attached to the wing leading edge and twin tailbooms carrying a vast elliptical tail unit, the 120-passenger load originally envisaged or freight were to be accommodated in cabins within the wing structure. To satisfy this design requirement, the huge wing-span was matched by an extraordinary chord of nearly 35 feet (10.6 m), allowing a maximum wing depth of 7 feet 8 inches (2.33 m).

Construction of the K-7 had begun in 1931, but only after the Soviet government had altered its role to that of very heavy bomber, typically carrying more than 32,000 pounds (14,500 kg) of bombs or a maximum

RIGHT
The giant Junkers G 38 airliner with wing cabins.

BELOW
Dyle & Bacalan DB 70 airliner in 1929, which led to bomber derivatives built by Bordelaise.
Philip Jarrett collection.

41,900 pounds (19,000 kg) in overload, while for defence guns were placed at the nose and in three positions on each tailboom. The giant, weighing up to a maximum of 93,475 pounds (42,400 kg), managed 140 miles per hour (225 km/h on six tractor and one pusher M-34F engines. Then, in November during a low altitude test flight, a tailboom failed and the K-7 plunged to the ground, killing all but five of the twenty on board. Although construction of two more K-7s was started, they were never completed.

A better-known builder of huge aircraft in the Soviet Union was Tupolev, whose TB-1 and TB-3 monoplane heavy bombers became standard equipment with the air force during the interwar period and were still in service as G-2 transport conversions and emergency night bombers when Germany invaded. Using all its experience to design an even larger monoplane for the unusual purpose of official government propaganda, Tupolev constructed the ANT-20MG *Maxim Gorki* that first flew on 19 May 1934 as the world's largest landplane. Six of its eight 900 hp M-34FRN engines were carried on the 206-foot 8-inch (63-m) wings, the remaining two being pylon-mounted in tandem above the fuselage. To meet its unusual role, cabins were provided for wireless operations, and for printing and filming, while illuminating gear permitted slogans to be displayed under the wings

while flying. Tragically, on 18 May 1935 the pilot of an escorting Polikarpov I-5 fighter decided to attempt a loop around the *Maxim Gorki*'s wing. He failed, striking the wing and causing both aircraft to drop out of the sky locked together. The I-5 pilot and all forty-five people on board *Maxim Gorki* were killed. Plans were in hand to produce sixteen more, but the operating unit was not keen on having them and instead the aircraft was redesigned into the ANT-20bis (PS-124) airliner for 64–85 passengers. The first airliner was completed in 1938 and began services between Moscow and Mineralnye Vody in 1940, but this was the only example completed. Turning later to war work, it was lost in 1942.

All at Sea

Some of the most interesting and unusual aircraft of the interwar period were giant flying-boats, intended to span seas and oceans on commercial services, typically crossing the larger expanses in stages. Indeed, the biggest of these monsters of the waves were strange because of their very proportions although, during this period, flying-boats were the only large commercial aeroplanes fully suited and safe for long over-water flights. The French Latécoère 521, for example, had a huge wingspan of 161 feet 9 inches (49.3 m) and first flew on 17 January 1935 on the power of six 860 hp Hispano-Suiza 12Ybrs tractor and pusher engines. For trans-Mediterranean flights it

The first Latécoère 521 giant flying-boat
Lieutenant de Vaisseau Paris.
Philip Jarrett collection.

could accommodate seventy passengers
(including six in sleeping compartments);
passenger numbers were reduced to thirty
for trans-Atlantic services.

The Laté 521 proved to be a highly
successful aircraft, although in 1936 it
suffered the indignity of sinking at its
moorings in Miami while on a circuit of the
Atlantic. Fortunately, it was not too badly
damaged and returned to France for
rebuilding, when the opportunity was also
taken to replace the original engines with
lower-rated Hispano-Suizas.

Of three more examples ordered for
commercial use, only the Laté 522 was
completed. This and the Laté 521 were
impressed by the French Navy at the
outbreak of war, but after only a few months
the Laté 522 was allowed to continue
passenger flying. Their final fate

came in 1944, when retreating Germans
destroyed them. Meanwhile, three fully-
military and armed Laté 523s had joined the
French Navy in 1938, capable of Atlantic
patrols of up to thirty-three hours duration.
One was sunk in September 1939, a second
was scuttled to prevent it falling into
German hands, and the last stopped flying
in 1942 after operations from Dakar.

Other more modern-looking six-engined
flying-boats followed the Laté 521 series,
including the 188-foot 5-inch (57.43-m)
wingspan Latécoère 631. Design had started
in 1938 as a forty-passenger trans-Atlantic
aircraft with a range of well over 3,700
miles (6,000 km), but construction was
temporarily halted by the outbreak of war.
Completed under German occupation, it was
seized by German forces and taken to
Friedrichshafen, where it was sunk by

32

(8.5 m) and at 123,460 pounds (56,000 kg) maximum take-off weight it was half as heavy again, requiring twelve 525 hp German-built Bristol Jupiter or later 600 hp Curtiss Conqueror engines to provide sufficient power. In flight, it consumed around 350 gallons (1,590 litres) of fuel every hour and yet could still manage 1,050 miles (1,700 km), although its designed stage lengths were less than this. Above all, the Do X stood for luxury, with an anticipated average load of forty to eighty passengers pampered in lavish surroundings within the 14,000 cubic foot (396.4 m³) hull. Of course, it could carry a much greater number of people if required, and on 21 October 1929 it actually took off with ten crew, 150 passengers and nine stowaways.

Despite a fairly good top speed of 134 miles per hour (216 km/h), the Do X proved to have a low ceiling of 1,640 feet (500 m) and was prone to trouble. Its best-remembered journey began at Friedrichshafen on 2 November 1930, the start of a staged publicity and proving flight to New York. Delays and mishaps that included a fire-damaged wing at Lisbon and hull damage sustained in the Canary Islands meant that New York was not reached until 27 August 1931. Two further New York flights were recorded; on 24 June 1932 it landed on the Muggelsee near Berlin after a 28,000-mile (45,000 km) tour of Europe and South and North America, an epic journey that had included two trans-Atlantic crossings. These flights aside, it was an impracticable aircraft and the two other Do Xs built for an Italian operator never saw commercial service and were taken over by the military for a brief period.

German flying-boats have other claims to fame. During the Second World War, the Blohm und Voss Bv 222 Wiking was the largest operational flying-boat of the war of any nation, while the company's follow-on Bv 238 of 1944 was the largest flying-boat built and flown during this conflict. With a wingspan of 197 feet 4 inches (60.15 m) and a weight of over 176,000 pounds (80,000 kg), it required six 1,750 hp Daimler-Benz

Allied bombers. After the war, a further nine Laté 631s were built by SNCA de Sud-Ouest, fitted with 1,600 hp or even more powerful Wright radial engines. Air France was to receive six, and trans-Atlantic services between Biscarrosse and Martinique began in July 1947. The great expectations were short-lived, however, when by 1948 two had been lost, forcing the withdrawal of the survivors from passenger routes. Freighting seemed a likely new purpose, and the eighth Laté 631 began commercial freighting in 1949 but was lost the following year. Without a role, the remaining flying-boats languished unused, some finally being destroyed inside their hangars during abnormal weather. Two of four contemporary French Sud-Est SE 200 six-engined flying-boats seized by the Germans during the Second World War

were also destroyed by the RAF, while the other two were launched after the war as eighty-passenger transports.

The double honour of being the largest aeroplane in the world at the time of its first flight on 25 July 1929, and of being the biggest and heaviest flying-boat to be completed between the wars, went to the remarkable German Dornier Do X. Conceived as a giant outgrowth of the Dornier Wal for trans-Atlantic commercial operations, this flying-boat actually achieved little of lasting value but it still managed to acquire almost as much notoriety in the aviation world as the highly successful German *Graf Zeppelin* intercontinental airship.

With wings of 157 feet 6 inches (48 m), its span was less than that of the Laté 521, but its overall length was greater by 28 feet

ABOVE
Early photograph of the Dornier Do X, the largest interwar flying-boat, with Jupiter engines in six tandem pairs.

OPPOSITE
Tupolev ANT-22 (MK-1) twin-hulled flying-boat. Via Russian Aviation Research Trust/G. Petrov.

engines. Tested on the Schaal lake, the prototype was destroyed by US Mustang fighters while at its moorings and no others were ever finished.

A strangely interesting Soviet concept for an ultra-large flying-boat appeared from Tupolev in 1934, when during that August manufacturer's trials started with the ANT-22 (MK-1). Conceived as a long-range

reconnaissance-bomber, it appeared at first sight to be the convenient marriage of two aircraft, the twin hulls joined by a thick centre-section wing that also carried the 13,225-pound (6,000-kg) bombload. Six M-34R engines were strut-mounted above the hulls and centre wing (in tandem pairs), while the pilots occupied a central nacelle on the wing leading edge. Six defensive gun

Hughes H-4 Hercules, or *Spruce Goose*, at 320 feet (97.5 m). The brainchild of multi-millionaire Howard Hughes, its design had begun in 1942 when Hughes joined forces with the shipbuilder, Henry Kaiser, to produce three ultra-large experimental flying-boats against an official US Navy/Government requirement. Accommodation was to be provided for 700 passengers or vast quantities of freight. Anticipating a possible future shortage of strategic metals, the aircraft was ordered to be of wooden construction.

Working on such a vast aircraft proved no simple task, and the inevitable delays took hold of the project. More crucial to officials, though, subassemblies were coming out overweight, which cast doubts on the likelihood of eventual success. As the expected national shortage of strategic metals did not occur either, there later seemed no good reason for the Aircraft and War Production Boards to continue supporting construction. Thus, in 1944, the plug was pulled on the programme, much to the annoyance of Hughes.

Rich and single-minded, Hughes decided to go it alone and prove the doubters wrong. He would complete just one H-4, spending a reported $22 million of his own wealth. So large were the

turrets were divided between the two hulls. Possessing a wingspan of 167 feet (51 m), the ANT-22 had good sea qualities but general performance fell short of expectations. Flying ended in late 1936 and no production was undertaken.

Larger still

In terms of wingspan, the largest aeroplane ever flown was another flying-boat, the

individual sections that road convoys using special trailers were organized in 1946 to transport these from Culver City where manufacturing had taken place to Long Beach (California) for final assembly. The H-4 weighed 400,000 pounds (181,436 kg), a truly incredible figure for the time, and required the power of eight 3,000 hp Pratt & Whitney R-4360 Wasp Major engines to lift.

Launched on 1 November 1947, the H-4 began immediate taxi trials in Los Angeles Harbor, with Hughes at the controls. The second run had shown the aircraft to be unexpectedly buoyant and so, although unscheduled, Hughes used the third run to attempt an actual flight. With no co-pilot but some thirty technicians and observers on board, the H-4 lifted out of the water for a flight of about one mile (1.6 km) at an altitude of some 75 feet (23 m). It is often said that Hughes made the flight to win a tiny wager. Whether or not this is so, Hughes announced that flying would not resume until March or April 1948. The aircraft was hangared and subsequently cocooned, never to fly again. In 1981 it was taken over for the Queen Mary and Spruce Goose exhibition in California and rehoused under a vast purpose-built dome.

The giant flying-boats from various nations had very mixed fortunes, and with the post-war advent of long-range landplanes the days for any large flying-boats on commercial routes were numbered. The splendid luxury of unhurried pre-war travel would never return.

This *end of an era* is perhaps best summed up by the fortunes of the British Saunders-Roe Princess, conceived in 1943 for post-war use and sanctioned in 1945 by the Ministry of Supply and BOAC as a 105-220-seater for a non-stop London-to-New York service. Unfortunately, even before the first prototype flew on 22 August 1952 in civil registration, BOAC had unofficially

1939 Boeing Model 314.

pulled out of the programme and the Princess had become a potential military freighter for the RAF. Of the three aircraft originally ordered, only two were ever completed, of which just the first was flown (for a total of nearly ninety-seven hours during forty-seven flights up to June 1954). The Princesses, those finished and incomplete, were subsequently cocooned against possible future sale, and right up to 1966 this seemed possible. However, when the final hope disappeared, the last of the Princesses (the flying prototype) was taken over by a breaker and part of its hull used as office space. The 219-foot 6-inch (66.9m) wingspan Princess remains, nevertheless, a quite remarkable milestone in aviation history, having been powered by no fewer than ten 3,780 shaft hp Bristol Proteus 2 turboprop engines, eight in coupled pairs.

Big flying-boats have appeared since but mainly for military use. Today Beriev

in Russia leads the world in such aircraft and has large jet-powered types both in service and under development. An earlier Beriev amphibian that does fit into the terms of this book, however, first flew on 4 September 1972 as the VVA-14 or M-62. Designed as the prototype for a large anti-submarine aircraft (three built), it featured a central fuselage carried above the water on two huge inflatable pontoons attached to nacelles under the deep centre-section wing. The outer wing panels were of high-lift design and of much higher aspect ratio. As the aircraft was expected to operate from land or water and be capable of short take-off and even vertical take-off, the two turbofan engines carried above the fuselage were joined by twelve RD-36 lift-jets in the fuselage.

Although the VVA-14 concept did not progress beyond trials, it formed the basis for the 14M1P ekranoplan (see the final chapter), which added two start engines at the nose and solid floats replaced the pontoons.

Piggybackers and Variations on a Theme
Smaller, conventional four-engined flying-boats of Boeing 314, Martin 130, Shorts Empire and similar types had proved highly successful commercial aircraft in the years leading up to the Second World War, though with much lighter loads than the contemporary giants had promised to provide. Even so, one of the greatest prizes had still to be won in the 1930s – that is, the establishment of regular non-stop commercial services across the North Atlantic between Britain and the USA. This

OPPOSITE,
ABOVE
Only one Saunders-Roe Princess flying-boat ever flew.

OPPOSITE,
BELOW
Beriev VVA-14 amphibian under tow. Via Russian Aviation Research Trust/G. Petrov.

BELOW
Remains of the Beriev 14M1P ekranoplan, with solid floats but outer wings and engines removed. Via Russian Aviation Research Trust.

39

distance was beyond the capability of these smaller aircraft and even regular scheduled trans-Atlantic services using staged stopping-off points did not begin until 1939.

Such a state of affairs led Shorts in the UK to fully develop a patented concept of Major R. H. Mayo, for a 'composite aircraft'. It was well-established knowledge that an aeroplane could maintain flight at a higher weight than that at which it could take off. It was also appreciated that fuel burned at take-off could only be restored through flight refuelling, a practice then still in its infancy. If, however, a long-range aircraft with full fuel and payload (and engines running) was helped into the air by a larger aircraft and then released, more fuel could be preserved and weight maximized. Thus the Short-Mayo Composite was born, with an S.20 twin-float seaplane named *Mercury* carried on a supporting and release structure above a fairly standard Empire flying-boat known as S.21 *Maia*. The first coupled flight took place on 20 January 1938 and the first separation followed shortly after on 6 February.

After a series of successful trials, the Composite was taken over by Imperial Airways on an experimental basis. The first commercial service was recorded on 21-22 July that same year when *Mercury*, having been launched by *Maia* after a combined take-off from Foynes in Ireland, flew to Montreal in Canada with 1,000 pounds (454 kg) of newspapers and photographs, the world's first commercial load carried non-stop across the North Atlantic by aeroplane. After refuelling, *Mercury* continued on to New York. The return flight had to be in stages. Other successful separations and epic flights followed, including one from Scotland to the Orange River in South Africa during 6-8 October 1938 to establish a world non-stop seaplane record of 5,997

Short-Mayo Composite, comprising S.20 twin-float seaplane Mercury *and lower S.21* Maia *flying-boat.*

ABOVE
Curtiss Sparrowhawk fighter hooking on to the lowered trapeze before being hoisted into USS Macon's *internal hangar.*

OPPOSITE, ABOVE
Zveno-2 experiments with a Tupolev TB-3 motherplane, overwing Polikarpov I-5s, underwing Polikarpov I-16s and central Grigorovich using a hook-on retrieval system. Via Russian Aviation Research Trust.

OPPOSITE, BELOW
Luftwaffe's Mistel composite manned fighter and unmanned expendable bomber unit.

miles (9,651 km). It was operating the Southampton-to-Alexandria service when the Second World War began and the flights ended. Imperial Airways' plan to operate other larger composites were thereby frustrated.

The demise of Short-Mayo Composite services was not the end of the 'piggyback' story. During the Second World War, the German Luftwaffe adopted a somewhat different approach to produce a guided flying bomb under its Beethoven-Gerät programme, better remembered by its later name of Mistel programme. In this, a piloted single-seat fighter was attached via a

structure to a multi-engined unmanned bomber which had been modified to carry a special high-explosive warhead. The pilot was then to fly the pair to the target and release the bomber for its final attack. Perfecting guidance proved difficult, however.

The first operational unit to receive Mistels was 2 Staffel of Kampfgeschwader 101, which was formed in April 1944. With a Messerschmitt Bf 109F-4 fighter and a Junkers Ju-88A-4 fitted with a 3,800-pound (1,725-kg) warhead comprising each Mistel I, the first action took place on 24-25 June 1944, when five attacked Allied ships

in the Seine Bay, where they were supporting the D-Day invasion. Other missions followed, Focke-Wulf Fw 190s later becoming the main upper element.

The Soviet Union also undertook composite operations during the war, when a number of Polikarpov I-16 fighters were converted into SPB dive-bombers, each with two 550-pound (250-kg) bombs, for air-launching in pairs from Tupolev TB-3 heavy bombers of the long-range Zveno unit operating over Romania and the Ukraine in 1941. This was the culmination of Zveno experiments that dated back to 1931, when a TB-1 bomber first air-released I-4 fighters

from its wings, followed by Zveno 2 experiments using TB-3s. But even these 'parasite fighter' trials were pre-dated by experiments in Britain and Germany in 1918 to air-launch fighters from airships, and in the USA parasite fighter trials as early as 1924 led to the world's first operational fighter-carrying airship, the USS *Akron*, used from 1931 to 1933 and accommodating four Curtiss F9C-2 Sparrowhawk fighters. Following the loss of *Akron*, USS *Macon* became home to the Sparrowhawks.

Post-war, a great many experimental and research aircraft were air-launched, sometimes because their power plants did

not permit a conventional ground take-off. Such was the case with the French Leduc experimental monoplanes, whose ramjet engines could not function until sufficient air velocity passed into their annular ducts.

In America, a bold attempt was made to continue the pre-war 'parasite fighter' concept, this time as part of the defence system for the new 230-foot (70-m) wingspan and six pusher-engined Convair B-36 intercontinental strategic bomber. The new atomic age required an equally modern fighter and so McDonnell produced the XF-85 Goblin jet. This tiny aircraft was built with a wingspan and length of only about

21 feet 3 inches (6.48 m) and 14 feet 10 inches (4.52 m) respectively, small enough with wings folded to fit into the front bomb-bay of the B-36. Power was provided by a 3,000-pound (1,360- kg) thrust Westinghouse J34-WE-22 turbojet engine, and launches and retrievals were to be conducted in mid-air using a retractable trapeze.

Trials with the Goblin began in 1948 using a modified Boeing B-29 bomber as the motherplane, with the first release on 23 August. For initial testing the Goblin had been provided with emergency landing skids. This proved a fortunate decision indeed, for after release and completing its first flight, the fighter approached the trapeze for retrieval but some instability and rough air made hook-on extremely difficult. Then, as the little fighter made another attempt, its canopy struck the trapeze with such force that it shattered and the pilot's helmet and oxygen mask were pulled off. Sucking just the oxygen hose, the pilot made a skilful emergency landing at 170 miles per hour (274 km/h). After the addition of wing fins to improve the Goblin's stability, a successful hook-on was managed on 14 October, and others followed. Despite these, the 520-miles-

per-hour (837 km/h) fighter was never adopted for operational B-36s.

Modern-day piggyback combinations include the six-turbofan Ukrainian Antonov An-225 Mriya freighter, used to ferry the Russian *Buran* space orbiter above its fuselage. The An-225 is currently the world's largest aircraft. Previously, a modified Boeing 747 (known as SCA - Shuttle Carrier Aircraft) had been prepared to carry the American Space Shuttle Orbiter in a similar manner. It was initially used to conduct a series of 'joined' aerodynamic tests and then, from 13 August 1977, to mid-air launch the Orbiter for its earliest free gliding test flights prior to the start of actual Shuttle space missions.

Chasing Speed

Air racing, since before the First World War, had been instrumental in encouraging clean and efficient aerodynamics, and keen rivalry between pilots and nations ensured this continued. The Deutsch de la Meurthe Cup held in 1919 was dominated by specially prepared versions of existing warplanes, namely the SPAD XX and Nieuport-Delage 29, and the Gordon-Bennett Aviation Cup held at Etampes in September 1920 saw the Ni-D29V winning once more. Of particular

ABOVE
Leduc 0.10 experimental ramjet aircraft that made its first powered flight on 21 April 1949 after being air-launched from above an SE 161 Languedoc airliner, displayed in the Musée de l'Air, Paris. Note the double-skinned fuselage, with the pilot's cockpit contained in the inner module and the outer skin forming the annular duct for the 4,400-pound (2,000-kg) thrust ramjet engine.
Austin J. Brown.

OPPOSITE,
ABOVE
Release of the McDonnell XF-85 Goblin from the B-29's trapeze on 23 August 1948.

INSERT
The Goblin with stablizing fins added to the wing tips.

BELOW
The Buran *space orbiter carried above the Antonov An-225.*
Austin J. Brown.

interest at Etampes, though, was another aircraft that nestled among the line-up of competing racers that failed to stay the course. This was the American Dayton-Wright RB. The Dayton-Wright Airplane Company had Orville Wright as its consulting engineer, and its RB racer embodied several unique features that made it both strange and innovative. In order to obtain the least possible drag, the undercarriage wheels were made to retract into wells in the fuselage sides, the high-mounted wing was of cantilever type requiring no external bracing struts or wires, and the pilot occupied a cockpit within the deep fuselage with only small side windows providing an outside view. Of even greater interest was the aircraft's variable camber mechanism for the wing, which could raise or lower the leading- and trailing-edges as required to alter the curvature, though it was problems with this system that caused the racer to retire from the event.

Racers with hugely powerful engines married to minimum-sized streamline airframes cropped up at various intervals throughout the interwar period. These impractical little machines had no other possible use than the attainment of speed. In 1923, the shapely but short and tailless Simplex designed by M. Arnoux made an appearance at Etampes. However, the most famous 'minimum' racers were the Gee Bees produced by the Granville brothers in the USA, and of these the strangest was the Super-Sportster. As prepared for the 1932 Thomson Trophy race, the 25-foot (7.62-m) wingspan Super-Sportster had an 800 hp Pratt & Whitney Wasp radial engine installed in a fuselage just 17 feet 9 inches (5.41 m) long and about 5 feet (1.52 m) deep, with the pilot seated just ahead of the small tailfin. Piloted by the famous aviator, James Doolittle, it won the event at an average speed of just above 252 miles per hour (405 km/h). Later it established a new world landplane speed record. For the 1933 National Air Races, the Super-Sportster was given a supercharged 900 hp Hornet engine. Tragically, Russell Boardman lost his life in the aircraft during the Bendix Trophy Race and the Granville Aircraft Corporation closed down that same year.

Not all 'minimum' racers were stumpy, though, and the (Harry) Crosby Special prepared for the 1936 National Air Races adopted a pencil-like fuselage to offer the smallest cross-section possible for a 300 hp supercharged Menasco Buchaneer inline piston engine. Indeed, such was the tiny depth of the tapering fuselage that the pilot had to sit in a semi-reclined position.

Of course, air racing continued up to the Second World War and after, despite the inevitable accidents, with designers and pilots willing to risk much for the

excitement, glittering prizes, records, accolades and more. Our modern times are no exception, although sometimes technologies have changed beyond recognition. Many of the most powerful piston-engined racers flown today are highly modified examples of Second World War fighters, able to achieve performances well beyond their original designers' expectations.

But, just now and then, something really special arrives to make heads turn. This was undoubtedly the case with the Pond Racer PR-01, produced by Scaled Composites in the USA, and intended not only for racing but to break the propeller-driven world speed record. The aim was to eventually exceed 530 miles per hour (853 km/h).

Because it was an entirely new design, not a modification, the Pond Racer could embrace advanced technologies from the outset. This it did with stunning results,

OPPOSITE, BELOW
Dayton-Wright RB racer at Etampes in 1920.
Philip Jarrett collection.

ABOVE
M. Arnoux's tailless Simplex racer of 1923.
Philip Jarrett collection/Photo-Rol.

BELOW
Granville brothers' Gee-Bee Super-Sportster.
Philip Jarrett collection.

N221BP

ABOVE
The highly original Pond Racer PR-01 produced by Scaled Composites.
Shawn Aro.

OPPOSITE
Stipa monoplane with a venturi duct fuselage.
Philip Jarrett collection.

becoming a very unusual twin-boom configuration, the pilot occupying a separate central nacelle with a special escape system. The wings swept forward, while the single main tailfin and rudder were joined by small 'butterfly' fins at the tailplane tips to enhance pitch and yaw stability. The Racer's structure used modern foam and carbonfibre composite materials to save weight, and power came from two Electramotive VG-30 turbocharged engines

with four-blade propellers, each rated at between 800 and 1,000 hp. First flown in 1991, actual racing at Reno began in 1992. Tragically, it was lost in an accident while preparing for the 1993 Reno event.

Stumpy airframes were not the sole domain of specialist interwar racers, however, and were not always provided just to house enormous engines. In the late 1920s, Dott. Ing. Luigi Stipa of the Italian Air Ministry conceived the idea of

producing an aeroplane with a venturi duct fuselage, having the engine and propeller inside the front orifice. It was believed that the slipstream from the orifice as it passed through the narrower tube of the hollow fuselage would increase total thrust. The overall height of the monoplane was 10 feet 8 inches (3.25 m), mostly entirely due to the fuselage diameter, although the aircraft's length was only slightly over 19 feet (5.8 m). Following wind tunnel tests, Caproni constructed the experimental prototype in 1932, sitting a 120 hp de Havilland Gipsy III engine. In trials the Stipa monoplane flew very well, and the extraordinary-looking fuselage is said to have contributed more than one-third of the required lift. Further experimentation on behalf of the Air Ministry continued therefore. ANF bought rights to permit experimentation in France, but little came of this.

Perhaps more than any other period in aviation history, the interwar years provided designers with opportunities to vent their full creativity in both commercial and military spheres, when so much had still to be learned and tested. After the Second World War, the most successful commercial aircraft generally stayed inside the boundaries of certain established parameters, although within this generalization several fascinating examples of the more extraordinary did appear, often to disappear just as quickly. But for military aircraft, anything still went!

Chapter Three
The Desperate Struggle

Germany's Third Reich at war provided the backdrop for many of the strangest aircraft, some born out of ingenious research or, later, desperation. Such was the number of advanced projects in hand in Germany that it was upon captured German technical information and prototypes (sometimes incomplete) that a good deal of post-war research in other countries was based, especially in the USA and Soviet Union, the Soviets taking greatest delight in Germany's rocket programmes, prototype jet bombers and turbojet engines.

Arguably the strangest of all aeroplanes flown during the Second World War was the Blohm und Voss Bv 141, resulting from a 1937 requirement calling for a short-range tactical reconnaissance machine capable also of army co-operation if required, to eventually supersede the Henschel Hs 126. To this requirement Dr-Ing Richard Vogt at Hamburger Flugzeugbau designed the Ha 141, an aeroplane of such unusual configuration that no official funding was provided for prototype construction. It was as a private venture, therefore, that the Ha 141 first flew on 25 February 1938.

The requirement had called for a three-seater, with outstanding all-round vision and a single engine offering about 850 hp at take-off. The Ha 141, as flown, seemed well placed to meet the specifications and was reluctantly short-listed by the RLM for further development as the Bv 141, the

designation reflecting Hamburger's new name of Blohm und Voss. In competition were the Arado Ar 198, a fairly conventional monoplane but featuring a heavily glazed ventral station built around the main fixed undercarriage legs, and the twin-boom Focke-Wulf Fw 189 Uhu that should have been rejected at the outset for having twin engines but was always the favoured aircraft.

The Bv 141 was an asymmetrical design, with a very heavily glazed crew nacelle set to the starboard side of a boom with both the engine and tail unit. The port wing attached to the boom was thus of greater span than the starboard wing attached to the nacelle, and a small centre section married the boom and nacelle, this arrangement countering the displaced centre of gravity. The position of the crew nacelle also went a long way in counteracting propeller torque. Unfortunately, although the original Ha 141 and three Bv 141V prototypes had been followed by five A series pre-production aircraft and then five B series aircraft with new asymmetric tailplanes, it was May 1943 before the last Bv 141B was delivered for trials, by which time the Fw 189 had been operational on the Eastern Front for a full year. Earlier service evaluation with Bv 141B-V10 in Saxony during late 1941 had led to immediate plans to form at least a single operational Bv 141 unit on the Eastern front, but this had been revoked in early 1942 as

Blohm und Voss Bv 141 asymmetrical reconnaissance and army co-operation aircraft.
Philip Jarrett collection.

some problems persisted.

The year 1937 also marked the genesis for another of Germany's stranger aircraft, the elegant and undervalued Dornier Do 335 Pfeil. In that year Dr-Ing Claudius Dornier took out a patent to protect his own 'centreline-thrust' concept, believing that a conventional nose-mounted engine and tractor propeller used in concert with a second engine to turn a shaft-driven pusher propeller mounted behind the tail unit was worthy of further research. Of course, twin-engined 'centreline thrust' aircraft had appeared before, and one of the earliest examples was the Siemens-Schuckert Dr I triplane fighter of 1917. However, a modern centreline-thrust aircraft with both engines in the fuselage and driving propellers at the extremities was unique. Most importantly, it provided the 'cleanest' possible airframe configuration for a twin-engined aircraft, minimizing drag.

To test the shaft-driven rear propeller concept, Schempp-Hirth was contracted to build a small experimental monoplane with a single 80 hp engine, as the Göppingen Gö 9. This flew in 1940. Encouraged by the success of Gö 9, Dornier produced a series of centreline-thrust fighter proposals but the RLM showed only passing interest as it wanted the company to concentrate on its already established and vital bomber and flying-boat work. Then, in 1942, the RLM outlined a requirement for a single-seat, very high-speed intruder, capable of

carrying 1,102 pounds (500 kg) of bombs. Dornier envisaged a centreline-thrust layout and its Project 231 was selected against competition, receiving the designation Do 335. However, soon after work began, changes in Germany's fortune led to a request to redesign the aircraft into a large heavy fighter, suited also to fighter-bomber, two-seat night-fighter and long-range reconnaissance roles.

The first of several prototype, pre-series and production Do 335s previously ordered flew in October 1943. A pre-series Do 335A-O fighter-bomber underwent initial operational evaluation in July 1944, allowing a unit to be formed for full evaluation that September. But slow delivery to Dornier of the 1,800 hp Daimler-

Benz DB 603 engines and other components from suppliers retarded the assembly programme. Such delays were to have severe consequences. As a result, just thirteen full production Do 335As had been completed when the factory was overrun by US forces, and this small total included two conversion trainers with tandem cockpits. Others, though, were in various stages of assembly. With a maximum speed of 474 miles per hour (763 km/h) it was one of the fastest piston-engined aircraft ever built and by far the fastest for the wartime Luftwaffe, and could have played a major role in Germany's defence had sufficient numbers been completed earlier. In the event, none is thought to have served with a fully operational unit.

Out with Propellers

As early as 1941 proposals were accepted to build turbojet-powered bombers in Germany, Arado taking the initiative with its twin-engined Ar 234 Blitz. Unfortunately, however, development of jet fighters and fighter-bombers received priority over pure bombers for early Junkers 109-004 turbojet engines, a situation made worse by protracted engine development that even frustrated Messerschmitt in its rush to get the Me 262 fighter airborne in turbojet form. Of course, Heinkel had been able to fly its He 280 twin-jet fighter as early as April 1941 because of its use of Heinkel HeS 8 turbojets, but this aircraft was subsequently abandoned in favour of the Me 262.

When Messerschmitt first flew an Me 262 prototype in turbojet configuration, on 18 July 1942, Arado became hopeful that its own starvation of jet engines was nearly over. It was wrong and the first Ar 234 was not to fly until 15 June 1943. The bomber was, however, a wonderful success.

The Blitz had been designed to fly high and fast, with the single pilot on an ejection seat in a pressurized cabin. With such a combination of attributes it was, indeed, a revolutionary aircraft, though it should be remembered that ejection seats had by then already become operational on the Heinkel He 219 piston night fighter and Henschel had been flying pressurized Hs 130 prototypes as early as 1940. Two development Arados were assigned to undertake the first actual operations, from 20 July 1944, though as unpressurized reconnaissance aircraft without ejection seats, while missions by actual Ar 234B-2 jet bombers began that December against Allied forces during the Ardennes offensive. Severe fuel shortages and the need to move units from one operating base to another as Allied forces closed in meant that many of some 250 Ar 234s built never found their way to operational units and so the full potential of this jet bomber was never fully realized.

Meanwhile, in 1943 Junkers had started work on a heavy strategic jet bomber, later to be designated Ju 287 and intended as a long-term replacement for the troublesome Heinkel He 177 that had earned the nickname 'flaming coffin'. Rival designs with W-planform wings came from Blohm und Voss, and Horten at some stage proposed a six-engined flying-wing bomber, while Junkers itself also drew up plans for a four-engined flying-wing, but only the Ju 287 proceeded. Interestingly, so critical became the need for a new large strategic bomber that, while still working on the Ju 287, Junkers proposed and had accepted in 1944 a plan to build the Ju 488 as a conventionally-powered four-engined bomber using some existing assemblies from current Junkers aircraft. However, in July 1944 French saboteurs wrecked the fuselages of prototype Ju 488s at Toulouse that were being prepared for transportation by rail to Bernberg, and the Ju 488 programme was abandoned that November.

For the Ju 287, Junkers decided to use radical forward-swept wings, which offered the advantages of sweptback wings but

meant that the worst handling characteristics came at high rather than low speeds. Two of the four Jumo 004 turbojets were wing-mounted, the others carried on the forward fuselage. This proposal was so far-reaching, however, that it was decided to test the configuration using a makeshift prototype, and so on 16 August 1944 Ju 287V1 flew as a concoction of an He 177 fuselage, Ju 388 tail and other borrowed parts that even included American B-24 Liberator nosewheels! Two jettisonable Walter rocket packs attached to the underwing engine nacelles boosted take-off, and the aircraft's undercarriage was non-retractable.

Even as a 'spare parts' prototype, Ju 287V1 recorded 347 miles per hour (558 km/h), reaching over 400 miles per hour (643 km/h) in a shallow dive. However, by July 1944 the need to adopt an all-embracing emergency fighter programme to avert pending German defeat led to the termination of bomber projects, only to be revived at the eleventh hour in 1945. Construction of a true Ju 287 in V2 prototype form with six BMW 003A-1 engines was thereby underway when the factory was captured by the Soviet army. The Ju 287V2 generated a great deal of interest and was sent back to the Soviet Union for completion, flying in 1947 but with sweptback wings. Only a small number of components for the six-engined Ju 287V3 derivative were then in evidence, which was to have had two of its engines at the fuselage nose, but it is worth noting that estimates put its likely maximum speed at 537 miles per hour (864 km/h) As for Ju 287V1, this had been virtually destroyed during an earlier Allied air raid.

The Luftwaffe's deployment of the Messerschmitt Me 262A-1a jet as the Schwalbe interceptor from July 1944 (followed by Me 262A-2a Sturmvogel fighter-bomber variant) resurrected hopes in Germany that something could be done to stem the debilitating effects of the Allied bomber offensive. Such confidence was boosted by the near simultaneous

deployment of the tiny single-seat Messerschmitt Me 163 Komet, the world's first operational rocket interceptor. Towards the end of July 1944, US bombers and escort fighters encountered Komets for the first time, but without loss to either side. During the course of the next few weeks, all operational Staffels of Jagdgeschwader 400 (the sole Komet unit) were concentrated at Brandis. But, as history recalls, only nine bombers ever fell victim to Komets and only about 300 Komets were built in total.

The Komet had first flown in prototype form in 1941, initially as a glider and then powered. It proved to possess a low gliding sink rate, while with rocket power (on 2 October) it attained over 623 miles per hour (1,000 km/h). The operational Me 163B had a 3,750-pound (1,700-kg) thrust Walter 109-509A-2 motor fuelled by T-Stoff (hydrogen peroxide and water) and C-Stoff (hydrazine hydrate, methyl alcohol and water). With this, a speed approaching 600 miles per hour (965 km/h) was possible, with an initial rate of climb of about 12,000–16,400 feet (3,660– 5,000 m) per minute. The penalty for such performance combined with a tiny airframe was a powered endurance of less than eight minutes.

There are a number of reasons why the Komet had so little impact on the war, not least of which were Allied bombing that disrupted manufacture and training, Allied advances curtailling the number of possible operational bases, difficulties with the motor and with fuel leaks, a general shortage of fuel, and armament shortcomings. The Komet had been manufactured for point defence, to scramble as enemy bombers were virtually overhead and climb past at very high speed, then to make either a gliding or powered attack from above. One difficulty came in hitting a bomber with just two 20-mm or 30-mm

Messerschmitt Me 163B-1 Komet. Note the skid, used for landing as the trolley wheels were jettisoned at take off.

cannon while closing in at over 300 miles per hour (480 km/h) greater speed, when the cannon range meant that the pilot had only two or three seconds to fire, and often the cannon jammed. Moreover, by having to concentrate operations at Brandis instead of the planned ring of sites, its usefulness was vastly diminished. Landing at 137 miles per hour (220 km/h) on a skid was no easy task, and a number of Komets exploded during touch-down accidents.

As mentioned before, by later 1944 matters for Germany were becoming critical. It was becoming obvious there would be neither the number of Me 262 and Me 163 interceptors needed, nor the basing requirements, to give any realistic hope of averting disaster. Strategic materials were also in extremely short supply. What was needed was yet another new high-performance fighter capable of outmatching

enemy piston-engined types, yet one requiring just a single precious engine, using little strategic materials in its construction, and so simple in layout that huge numbers could be turned out quickly by unskilled and semi-skilled labour. As importantly, it had to be easy to fly, as Goering believed boys of the Hitler Youth who proved capable glider pilots could be trained to fly the fighter, though the first operational aircraft were to go to experienced Luftwaffe pilots.

In early September 1944 an official requirement was issued for such a Volksjäger (People's Fighter), with several companies proposing designs, though not Messerschmitt. One week was all that could be spared for initial proposals. Heinkel had previously conceived a lightweight fighter as the Spatz and this was a useful starting point for its Project 1073. A mock-up was displayed on 20 September, it was selected on the 23rd, and a contract was received on the 29th (as the He 162 Salamander). Amazingly, a prototype first flew on 6 December, just 69 days after the contract date, though it crashed on the 10th.

Fifty He 162s were wanted in January 1945, 100 in February and then up to 1,000 each month, but in January very few had been readied. With the Allies' relentless advance, factories had to close and airfields were abandoned. By 4 May Einsatz-Gruppe JG 1 forming at Leck was the only He 162 unit still in operation, its fifty or so aircraft having very little fuel with which to fly. Surrender followed four days later. Some 116 He 162s had joined the Luftwaffe from nearly 300 completed but these had hardly ever been seen by Allied pilots. With a wooden airframe, a single 1,765-pound (800-kg) thrust BMW 109-003E turbojet mounted above the fuselage and two 20-mm cannon, it nevertheless had met many of the original requirements, but at the penalty of being fairly unstable and requiring careful piloting.

Manned Missiles

In addition to fighters, Germany had been working on surface-to-air missiles for several years. The Henschel Hs 117 Schmetterling, as the most developed, was ordered into mass production in December 1944, with anticipated initial operational deployment from the first launch site in about March 1945. It was hoped that 3,000 missiles per month could be coming off production lines by late 1945. In the event, none became operational. A curious marriage between interceptor and missile technologies, however, led to another of Germany's strangest aircraft, the Bachem Ba 349 Natter.

The Natter was conceived as a semi-expendable, rocket-powered and piloted point defence interceptor, using a more powerful version of the Me 163B's motor (as intended for the Me 163C) plus two or four solid-fuel rocket boosters. Launched from a near-vertical structure, it was to fly under autopilot until within a short distance of the enemy bomber formation, when the pilot would take control for final guidance to target and jettison the nosecone to expose

twenty-four Hs 217 73-mm Föhn unguided rockets to be fired in one salvo at the enemy. The pilot was then to discard the entire nose of the Natter (together with the simple cockpit) and bale out, the rear fuselage returning to ground by separate parachute for reuse.

The first piloted launch of a Natter on 28 February 1945 ended in tragedy. Soon after clearing the launch structure, the aircraft's canopy detached unexpectedly. The Natter then turned over and continued a slow climb to nearly 5,000 feet (1,525 m) before diving to the ground, the pilot losing his life. Successful launches in March, however, led to the decision to deploy ten at Kirchheim in April, to intercept US bombers. Although readied for use, Allied ground forces captured the site before any were launched in anger. With only seven ever flown with pilots on board and eighteen flown as unmanned aircraft during trials, the Natter was of absolutely no use whatsoever to either Luftwaffe or SS units.

Japan's purpose-designed Yokosuka MXY-7 Ohka rocket-powered suicide aircraft, deployed from March 1945, is fairly well known. Less familiar are Germany's Fieseler Fi 103R and Messerschmitt Me 328, conceived for self-destruction in pinpoint attacks on high-value land and sea targets should the Allies launch an invasion of Europe. The principal operating difference between the German and subsequent Japanese aircraft was that German pilots had a slight chance of baling out from the doomed machines just before impact, though in reality this was extremely slim.

The Fi 103R was virtually a manned conversion of the V1 flying-bomb, intended for air-launching from a bomber. Some 175 were built but the plan was dropped in favour of the Mistel composite. The Me 328 was a more advanced concept, intended to be powered by two underwing Argus pulse jets or to be air-launched as a glider, in either case carrying a 1,102- or 2,204-pound (500- or 1,000-kg) bomb externally. This project, too, was abandoned.

Giant Gliders

Immediately following Germany's postponement of 'Operation Sealion' (the invasion of Britain) in October 1940, Junkers and Messerschmitt were approached to design in haste giant armed transport gliders that could be used in a future invasion for carrying heavy armoured vehicles, guns, supplies or troops as part of an airborne assault force. Such was the anticipated urgency that 200 examples of both the Ju 322 Mammut and Me 263 Gigant were ordered into production that November, the Messerschmitt later redesignated Me 321.

With a wingspan of 181 feet 3 inches (55.25 m) and weighing 77,160 pounds (35,000 kg) at take-off when loaded or up to 86,862 pounds (39,400 kg) at overload weight, the Me 321 became the largest operational glider of the Second World War, its metal tubing, wood and fabric fuselage having a cargo space of approximately 36 feet (11 m) length, 11 feet (3.3 m) height and 10 feet (3.15 m) width. A 44,092-pound (20,000-kg) load could be carried, accessed through clamshell doors that formed the entire nose section, or up to 200 troops.

The Me 321 was first towed into the air by a Junkers Ju 90 on 25 February 1941, but while the glider performed well, the towing aircraft struggled to meet its task. Revised plans later provided for a Ju 290 or, as became standard, three Messerschmitt Bf 110 fighters towing each Me 321. In June 1941 the first Grossraum-Lastenseglergruppe unit was formed, with each of three Me 321 Stafeln having six gliders and each of three towing aircraft Stafeln having 12 Bf 110s. The ultimate solution to the towing problem, however, came with the development of another strange aircraft in its own right, the Heinkel He 111Z Zwilling. This comprised two He 111H bombers joined at the wings and carrying a fifth engine. He 111Zs became available in mid-1942, but by then the Me 321 force had been reduced pending the introduction of the self-powered Me 323.

Me 321s were first used on the Eastern Front, where they undertook logistic support missions. But as the weather deteriorated, the use of triple-towing Bf 110s became unsafe and operations were restricted in later 1941 and then postponed in early 1942 pending their use in the invasion of Malta; introduction of the He 111Z placated the towing problem and this aircraft was to be used for the Malta operations. In the event, the invasion was abandoned along with several other operations, and Me 321s became locally available too late to help in the resupply of German forces at Stalingrad in 1943. Missions thereafter became fewer.

The towing difficulties had already led to the decision to develop a powered variant of the Me 321, beginning with the conversion of two Me 321s, the first with four engines and the second with six. Flight trials started in the early spring of 1942. Production Me 323Ds and Es entered service

from late 1942, each powered by six 1,140 hp Gnome-Rhône 14N 48/49 radial engines. While gross weight increased over the Me 321, the number of troops that could be carried fell to 120-130. Nearly as many Me 323s were produced as Me 321s, used to support the Afrika Korps from late 1942 but suffering heavy losses both on the ground and in the air from Allied warplanes. Despite considerable cannon armament for self-defence, the Me 323s flying at around 130 miles per hour (210 km/h) were easy targets. Many Me 323s finished their careers undertaking logistic and evacuation missions on the Eastern Front, until mid-1944.

Meanwhile, Junkers had faired somewhat less successfully with its Ju 322 Mammut. Unfortunately for the company, it had received the official specification for the all-wooden glider (the Me 321 was required to use a steel tube structure), but had little experience in the major use of such material. Junkers configured the Ju 322 as a flying-wing with a span of 203 feet 5 inches (62 m), though a boom-type fuselage was provided to carry the conventional tail. The deep centre section of the wing doubled as the cargo area, accessed via detachable leading-edge panels. The cockpit was offset to port, and three gun turrets provided

defence. In the event, the wooden structure, together with the quality of the material provided, meant that payload came out at 20 percent lower than required. Then, during loading tests, a battle tank compacted the cargo floor. A strengthened floor had therefore to be designed, reducing possible payload by about another 22 percent.

Flight trials were scheduled for April 1941, and a Ju 90 was assigned as the towing aircraft. There followed a series of near disasters. The Ju 90 struggled to pull the glider into the air before the runway ran out. Then, soon after take-off, the glider's jettisoned undercarriage trolley smashed on the ground, rebounding fragments on to the glider. Under tow, the glider proved highly unstable, quickly gaining height above the Ju 90 and so pulling the towplane's tail up and preventing it from climbing. Realizing the imminent danger to both aircraft, the glider pilot released the line, at which point the Ju 322 stabilized and landed safely on its skids but away from the launch field. It took two weeks for the glider to be towed back by tanks, as a suitable passage had to be prepared. Although Junkers set about some redesign, in May the project was cancelled and the ninety-eight other Ju 322s then under construction or virtually finished were cut up for firewood.

Interestingly, despite the RAF's warding off a German invasion of Britain in 1940, Britain, like Germany, believed this to be only a temporary postponement, making preparations for the defence of the British Isles still of vital importance. Among schemes put forward for straffing German forces as they hit British beaches or for striking at supporting surface vessels was the Westland P12, a straight modification of the Lysander army co-operation aircraft. Initially planned with two 20-mm cannon attached to the fixed undercarriage legs, a redesign led to the rear fuselage being cut short, a tail gun turret added, and the adoption of a new rear-mounted 'tandem wing' with endplate fins and rudders for longitudinal stability. The P12 was first flown on 27 July 1941 and was immediately shown to be highly manoeuvrable. Sent for official trials, it was never put into production as the perceived threat diminished.

ABOVE
Junkers Ju 322 Mammut giant wooden transport glider.

RIGHT
Westland P12 tandem-wing beach-straffing aircraft.

The Allies

It is correct to say that operational aircraft built by the Allies during the Second World War were generally less 'strange' than the hand-picked German types described earlier. The Allies had not been forced to implement late in the war an emergency fighter programme to stave off twenty-four hour strategic bombing, and had not attempted to explore fully many of the advanced technologies deemed viable and necessary to German planners. Of course, the British Gloster Meteor jet fighter was fielded at almost the same time as the German Me 262 (in 1944), and in the USA the Bell P-59 Airacomet entered USAAF service later that same year on the back of initial British jet engine technology transfer, although the Airacomet was principally used in very small numbers for training.

The Allies were not totally devoid of unusual projects, though. For, whilst it was left to Germany (and in some cases Japan) to field radical operational aircraft, experimental prototypes appeared elsewhere (particularly in the USA) that can be termed unconventional.

Several piston-engined experimental fighters were built for trials with the USAAF during the Second World War that were intended to investigate more radical configurations. Among the most revolutionary was the Curtiss XP-55 Ascender, with rear-mounted sweptback wings and winglets, small canards, and a 1,275 hp Allison V-1710 piston engine installed in the rear fuselage to drive a three-blade pusher propeller. Armament comprised two 20-mm cannon and four 0.50-inch machine-guns. The first of three prototypes flew on 13 July 1943. The XP-55 attained 390 miles per hour (628 km/h) but was not put into production.

Seemingly less radical was the Vultee XP-54 fighter, of which two prototypes were built, the first flying on 15 January 1943. Powered by a 2,300 hp Lycoming XH-2470-1 engine, it was intended to adopt contra-rotating pusher propellers. The wings were of cranked design, while the pilot sat on an ejection seat in a pressurized cockpit.

From Northrop came the XP-56 (manufacturer's designation N-2B), another pusher type with a 2,000 hp Pratt & Whitney R-2800-29 piston engine and contra-rotating propellers. The wings of this fighter had anhedral outer panels, while the tail surfaces comprised only dorsal and ventral fins. Control was affected by spoilers on the upper and lower surfaces of the anhedral panels and by elevators on the wing trailing edges. Two were built, the first flown on 30 September 1943.

An unusual US fighter originating in the Second World War that did enter production (although it was mainly used post-war) was the North American P-82 Twin Mustang, conceived for very long-range missions in the Pacific theatre. This warplane was principally for escort and night fighter roles (270 production aircraft) and was based on the marriage of two P-51 Mustang fighters, joined at the wings and tail and carrying two pilots. An F-82G (redesignated in 1948) was responsible for gaining the first American air victory of the Korean War, on 27 June 1950, over a North Korean Yak-9.

Probably the most original Allied fighter concept of the war was the Chance Vought F5U Skimmer. This, intended as a naval fighter, was to possess the widest possible speed range, from possible stationary or slow hover to 425 miles per hour (684 km/h), providing an ability to loiter. To achieve this seemingly impossible task, the two 1,350 hp Pratt & Whitney R-2000 Twin Wasp piston engines were to drive four-blade propellers with articulated blades, to perform as helicopter rotor blades when the aircraft assumed a high angle of attack, while a roughly circular wing-cum-fuselage accommodated the crew behind glazed panels. Armament was to be four 20-mm cannon and six 0.50-in machine-guns, with provision for two 1,000-pound (454-kg) bombs.

To provide data for the XF5U-1 prototypes, a small-scale demonstrator of wood and fabric was built as the V-173.

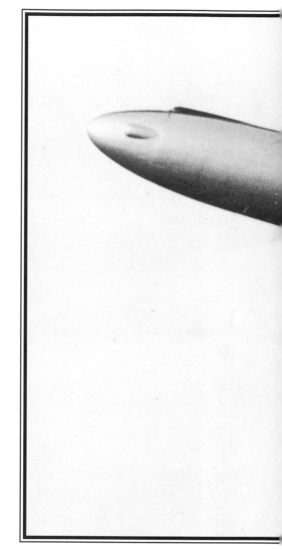

This was powered by two 80 hp Continental C80 piston engines. This first flew on 23 November 1942. Eventually, two full-size prototype fighters were ordered but only one was completed for testing at Muroc in 1947, and even this was never flown.

ABOVE
Vultee XP-54 pressurized fighter.

RIGHT
Chance Vought V-173 small-scale Skimmer demonstrator.
Philip Jarrett collection.

Chapter Four
Winged and Wingless

'Flying-wing' aeroplanes (those without conventional fuselages) have a history as old as powered flight itself, and yet a modern example has become the USAF's latest strategic bomber and the most technologically advanced production aeroplane ever built, and the most expensive at $2,114 million each!

A strong connection with the military has also been part of the flying-wing's history, although there are some notable exceptions. In Britain in 1904, Lieutenant John Dunne began theoretical work on an inherently stable aeroplane which, in 1905, led to the decision to construct a full-size glider, intended later to undertake powered trials after appropriate modification. At that time Dunne was a designer of man-carrying kites at the British Army's Balloon Factory in Farnborough, work he shared with the famous Samuel Franklin Cody. He was, therefore, well placed to receive official attention, and indeed such interest in this aeroplane project meant that construction of the D1 glider was government-financed and undertaken in strict secrecy: for testing in 1907 the Marquis of Tullibardine permitted his Scottish estate to be used as an isolated proving ground, though word still got out to foreign spies.

Dunne's concept was a biplane with vee-shaped swept superimposed wings, with 'wash-out' to ensure that the angle of

incidence became negative at the tips for the greatest possible stability. Ill-health from service during the Boer War meant that Dunne was unable to fly the glider himself. Following an accident during a short flight, the decision was taken to repair the airframe and modify it to a powered aeroplane, though the 7.5 hp of each of two engines officially provided was insufficient for take-off, even when using a downward inclined ramp. After sustaining more damage caused by the launching method during desperate attempts to make the machine fly on such little power, the D1 was again modified, becoming the D4 in

1908 with a 25 hp motor, pilot's nacelle, wingtip fins and a fixed four-wheel undercarriage. Even the new REP engine had too little output and the D4 struggled to achieve anything more than very brief hops. When official backing was withdrawn, Dunne left the Balloon Factory, taking the D4 with him.

The aircraft manufacturer Short Brothers built Dunne's D5, sponsored by the Blair Atholl Aeroplane Syndicate that had been formed to finance the aircraft by the Marquis of Tullibardine. With a 60 hp engine driving twin pusher propellers, it first flew in 1910 and could fly level

BELOW
Westland-Hill Pterodactyl Mk 1B.

without direct pilot control. Other machines followed, including the D5 rebuilt after an accident as the D8, in which in 1913 a French pilot left the controls and walked out on to the wing during a flying display, a brave act of faith in the machine's inherent stability.

The Pterodactyls

In Britain in the 1920s, Captain G.T.R. Hill conceived a tailless aircraft design with a wing section possessing a stationary centre of pressure, thereby allowing the aircraft to be controlled and manoeuvred even under stall conditions, while a high degree of lateral stability at slow speed came from adopting wing sweepback. Known as the Pterodactyl, the concept was taken up by Westland Aircraft for a series of experiments that lasted well into the 1930s. Following glider trials, the powered Mk 1A was built and proved wonderfully controllable during tests in 1926. It was

just the first Pterodactyl to be taken over by the British Air Ministry. A variant with a more-powerful 80 hp engine became the Mk 1B, while the subsequent Mk IV introduced an enclosed cabin for three persons. Particularly interesting was the Mk V sesquiplane, which was built in the early 1930s as an experimental two-seat fighter, with a 600 hp Rolls-Royce Goshawk engine in the nose and a rear-gunner's position.

Whilst the powered Dunne and Westland-Hill types were really tailless aircraft rather than true flying-wings, and certainly Viktor Belyayev's attempt in the Soviet Union to produce an inherently stable long-range bomber as the twin-fuselage and forward-swept wing DB-LK of 1939 was definitely not (as it is sometimes claimed to be) a flying-wing, aircraft of truly 'flying-wing' configuration had by then appeared.

Reappearance of Gotha Bombers

A most remarkable series of unpowered and powered flying-wing aircraft can be attributed to Reimar and Walter Horten in Germany, although their first Ho I glider of 1931 was exceptional only in being somewhat less than successful. Four examples of the improved Ho II glider followed, the pilot again adopting a prone position to ensure that only a shallow streamlined canopy spoiled the wing profile. One Ho II was later installed with an 80 hp Hirth engine and flown in powered form in 1935. All further Hortens up to and including the Ho VI were gliders, whose pilots included the famous German woman test pilot Hanna Reitsch, with the exception of the two-seat Ho V that flew in 1938 with two Hirth engines. The Ho VII with two 240 hp Argus As 10 engines remained another prototype, though at one time it had been seriously considered as suitable for flight-training duties.

By far the most important Horten therefore became the Ho IX, on which work began in 1942 as a single-seat jet-powered day fighter. The first airframe had almost been completed when the two BMW 109-003A-1 engines arrived for installation. Unfortunately, these engines were larger than anticipated and, to everyone's horror, would not fit between the aircraft's spars. Thus, V1 was tested as a glider in 1944. Meanwhile, Ho IXV2 was redesigned to adopt two highly-developed Junkers 109-004B-1 turbojets (although of even larger diameter), with which a staggering speed of nearly 500 miles per hour (800 km/h) was attained in early 1945 before it was lost in an accident, having managed just two hours accumulated flying time. Notwithstanding the setbacks, such was the potential of the Horten flying-wings that in the previous summer the Ho IX development programme had been officially transferred to Gotha, under the new designation Go 229, when seven more prototypes and twenty pre-production aircraft had been ordered. V3 became a prototype fighter-bomber and was virtually ready for flight testing when the

factory site was overrun by US forces. V4 was to have been the first two-seat day and night fighter variant, and V7 a tandem two-seat trainer. Maximum estimated speed for the Go 229A was 607 miles per hour (977 km/h), and armament for the fighter-bomber was four 30-mm cannon and two 2,204-pound (1,000-kg) bombs.

A non-military Horten flying-wing design had been the Ho VIII, intended as a sixty-passenger airliner, although as construction of the 157-foot (48-m) wingspan prototype had begun only after the war started, it would not have remained a commercial aircraft if completed in time. As designed, power was to come from six 600 hp BMW piston engines buried inside the profile, driving pusher propellers. In the event the war ended well before the

Ho VIII was finished, but this was not the end of the story. After the war, Reimar Horten assisted in the design and construction of the I.A.38 cargo transport in Argentina, based on the Ho VIII but with a span of 105 feet (32 m), having also a deep fuselage nacelle for six tons of cargo and powered by four 450 hp I.A.16E1 Gaucho piston engines. First flown on 9 December 1960, the project was eventually cancelled.

Never lose faith

In the USA, Northrop had been researching along similar lines, allowing the company to test in 1940 its N-1M flying-wing as a 38-foot (11.6-m) wingspan scale technology demonstrator for a projected large twin-engined transport. For early testing, the wing had been given anhedral tips to duplicate the functions of conventional

ABOVE

Northrop N-1M technology demonstrator, with original anhedral wingtips and two 65 or (later) 120 hp piston engines.

LEFT

Northrop N-9M, three of the four built each having two 275 hp Menasco piston engines, the fourth 300 hp Franklins.

vertical surfaces, but the aircraft proved too stable in flight and so appropriate modifications were made. N-1M eventually accumulated over 200 test flights and was easily the most successful true flying-wing powered aircraft up to that time.

There was no disguising the possibilities of the flying-wing layout for military aircraft and in September 1941 Northrop approached the USAAF with the general parameters for a large long-range medium bomber. Aided by the Wright Field Engineering Division, Northrop initiated detailed design work in 1942 on what was to become the four-engined XB-35. Before construction of two prototypes began in 1943, the company first produced a full-scale mockup and four 60-foot (18.3-m) span twin-engined scale aircraft as N-9Ms to provide technical data and familiarize pilots in flying-wing operations. The N-9Ms were highly successful and amassed many hundreds of flying hours.

The first XB-35 proper was not

completed at Northrop's Hawthorne works until 1946, but it was then the most radical bomber in existence. At 172 feet (52.4 m) span, and built as a single structure, it had the pilot occupying a cockpit with a fighter-style canopy offset from the centreline, while five other crew took up positions to his rear within the deep wing centre-section. A seventh crew member sat in a fire-control tail blister, to aim four remotely-controlled two-gun turrets positioned above and below the mid-span. To the defensive armament was added four-gun turrets above and below the centreline.

At 209,000 pounds (94,800 kg) take-off weight, the XB-35 had a useful load of 73,000 pounds (33,110 kg). Four 3,000 hp Pratt & Whitney R-4360 Wasp Major piston engines with turbosuperchargers turned contra-rotating pusher propellers.

First flown on 25 June 1946, when it flew to Muroc for Air Force trials, the first prototype was followed by the second XB-35 with single (instead of contra-rotating) propellers. After extensive evaluation, eight development YB-35s and five YB-35As were ordered. Their success led to a further order for 200 production B-35As, placed with Martin, but this order was cancelled before any of the aircraft had been built.

Meanwhile, it had been decided to convert two YB-35s into jet bombers under the new YB-49 designation, each with eight 4,000-pound (1,814-kg) thrust Allison J-35-A-5 turbojets in two groups of four, with leading-edge intakes providing air for the engines. Dorsal and ventral fins were added each side of the engine groups, and the gun blisters disappeared. With the jet engines, speed rose to 520 miles per hour (837 km/h). A third YB-35 had also been modified into the YRB-49 reconnaissance-bomber, first flown on 4 May 1950 with four 5,600-pound (2,540-kg) thrust J-35-A-21 turbojets in the wing trailing-edges and two in underwing pods. Thirty production RB-49s were ordered but these, too, were later cancelled.

Returning to 1944, in that year Northrop had fitted an Aerojet XCAL-200 rocket motor to its MX-324 flying-wing glider, first flown on 5 July as the first-ever US military rocketplane. This experiment was so sensitive that it remained a closely guarded military secret until 1947. Born out of this project was the XP-79B, a 38-foot (11.58-m) wingspan fighter using two 1,150-pound (520-kg) thrust Westinghouse 19B (J-30) turbojet engines to provide a speed of 510 miles per hour (820 km/h). Although armed with four 0.50-inch machine-guns, the wing was built of welded magnesium plate and as such was strong enough to ram or slice through the tails of enemy bombers, hence its unofficial name of Flying Ram. The pilot occupied a prone position in the well-glazed cockpit, the position being chosen not only to maintain the slim wing profile but help the pilot withstand the impacts of combat. Ducts at the wingtips provided air for the bellows-operated split horizontal control surfaces. The one and only XP-79B was to have a very short career, however, as only fifteen minutes into its first flight on 12

September 1945 the aircraft went out of control and was lost.

Interestingly, like Horten with the Ho VIII, Northrop too had planned a commercial airliner variant of its bomber. This B-49 derivative offered forty-eight main deck seats, various other main deck facilities, and an upper deck lounge in the area previously occupied by the bomber's fire-control blister.

It had been a shock when production of the large Northrop flying-wings was cancelled, especially as the YB-49 could cover distances of well over 3,450 miles (5,550 km) at a speed of 382 miles per hour (614 km/h), or 2,258 miles (3,633 km) at an average 511 miles per hour (822 km/h). Yet the company's faith in the flying-wing concept was never shaken, and when in 1978 it was announced that a new bomber was to be developed for the USAF for strategic penetration missions, Northrop submitted a radical new flying-wing design.

Eventually becoming the Northrop

Grumman B-2 Spirit, this bomber was intended from the outset for stealth operations (correctly termed low-observable), making its detection extremely difficult. A principal aim was to ensure that it offered the smallest possible radar image to an enemy, whereby the honeycomb internal structure, skin materials and special finishes absorb and dissipate rather than reflect radar energy. The composites materials used in its construction also greatly reduce infra-red signature, aided by the overwing air intakes and overwing engine exhaust nozzles. Tell-tale contrails left in the sky are reduced by management of the engine efflux temperature, while special avionics systems include the deployment of a 'low-probability-of-intercept' strike radar, and emitters are turned off when the aircraft goes into attack mode. To ensure that the airframe is 'clean' and so stealthy and efficient, all weapons are carried internally (up to 40,000 pounds/18,145 kg in two bays in the centre fuselage

NORTHROP Flying Wing Bomber

area, with weapons carried on racks or rotary launchers). Similarly, there are no vertical stabilizing or control surfaces, the jagged wing trailing edge having a series of horizontal elevons and split surfaces that undertake the work of ailerons, elevators, flaps, rudders and airbrakes.

The first of six B-2 development aircraft flew on 17 July 1989 as its delivery flight to Edwards Air Force Base (former Muroc). It had been expected that the USAF would eventually receive a total of 133 operational B-2As but cutbacks reduced this to twenty, of which sixteen are being operated by the 393rd and 715th squadrons of the 509th Bomb Wing at Whiteman AFB, achieving initial operational capability in 1997. In 1996 it was decided to fund the modification of the first B-2 development aircraft to bring it up to full operational standard, thereby giving the USAF twenty-one aircraft. The 172-foot (52.4-m) span B-2A has a take-off weight of 336,500 pounds (152,630 kg) and can cruise at Mach 0.8. Range with a 32,000-pound (14,515-kg) bombload is 6,900 miles (11,100 km), which

can be extended to over 11,500 miles (18,500 km) with flight refuelling.

Stealth technology is itself not new, having first been applied at Lockheed's secret 'Skunk Works' to operational aircraft for the USAF in the 1960s, used in the design of the SR-71 Mach 3 strategic reconnaissance aircraft (and its YF-12 interceptor counterpart that remained in

OPPOSITE
Northrop B-35 internal layout. Note the contra-rotating propellers and gun blisters.

ABOVE
Northrop XP-79 'Flying Ram' jet fighter.

BELOW
Northrop YB-49 flying-wing bomber.

ABOVE
Two-crew flight deck of the Northrop Grumman B-2A Spirit, although a third person can be accommodated.

OPPOSITE,
ABOVE
Northrop Grumman B-2A Spirit flying-wing bomber.

OPPOSITE,
BELOW
Lockheed YF-12A prototype Mach 3 interceptor.

prototype form) that first appeared in 1964, and more recently featured in the XST *Have Blue* technology demonstrators that led to the company's F-117A Nighthawk stealth fighter. Fifty-nine F-117As were taken into USAF service from 23 August 1982 as the world's first operational aircraft fully to exploit this 'low observable' or stealth technology.

Intended primarily to penetrate dense enemy environments at night, and attack high-value targets with great accuracy, the F-117A was designed to overcome seven signatures that could otherwise give away its position to an enemy, namely radar, infra-red, visual, contrails, engine smoke, acoustic and electromagnetic emissions, thereby remaining virtually 'invisible' and undetectable. The most obvious feature is its almost 'lifting-body' (see following paragraphs) facetted airframe, comprising many angled skin plates intended to reflect

an incoming radar beam away from its source, assisted by radar-absorbing edges and coatings. The possibility of infra-red detection is reduced by the use of non-afterburning engines and efflux cooling, above-wing air intakes and shielded exhaust nozzles of 'platypus' slot type that hasten contrail dispersal. In 1996 some fifty-three F-117As remained in USAF service.

Look – No Wings!

The same two United States manufacturers that had been involved to a large or small extent in the all-wing bomber programmes, namely Northrop and Martin Marietta, also worked on wingless 'lifting body' research aircraft during the 1960s to help NASA and the USAF evaluate the general concept for future space shuttle craft capable of transporting men and material to orbiting space stations and return to Earth for a conventional landing and reuse. Although individual aircraft were the designs of

NASA or the USAF and contracted out to the separate manufacturers, all were part of a joint NASA-USAF general programme. As time would show, the tiny aircraft provided much aerodynamic and other data vital to the eventual development of the US Space Shuttle Orbiter reusable spacecraft.

NASA teamed with Northrop, initially producing the M2-F1 unmanned wooden lifting-body glider for testing, followed by the piloted metal M2-F2 which had been an Ames Research Center concept. The tiny M2-F2 had a D-shaped cross section, with flaps on the upper and lower surfaces for pitch and roll control and others on the fins to control yaw. It made the first of sixteen unpowered flights on 12 July 1966 after being dropped from the wing of a B-52 bomber, proving that it could make a controlled descent and land safely on a runway. After the fourteenth flight an 8,480-pound (3,846-kg) thrust Thiokol XLR 11 rocket motor was installed, though not used immediately. However, on the sixteenth unpowered flight, on 10 May 1967, the M2-F2 made a wheels-up landing and was heavily damaged. It was reconstructed as the M2-F3 with an extra central fin, conducting powered tests from November 1970 until 1972.

Even before M2-F2 gliding flights began, Northrop had delivered to NASA a second lifting-body vehicle as the HL-10. This was somewhat different in design, having the flat edge of the D section on the underside, allowing the cockpit to be faired into the top-decking profile. It had a central fin and rudder from the outset, of larger size than that later fitted to M2-F3. HL-10 first flew unpowered on 22 December 1966 and by 1971 had completed twelve unpowered and twenty-five powered flights, reaching an altitude of 90,300 feet (27,525 m) and a speed of Mach 1.861. The motor used was

Lockheed F-117A Nighthawks, the world's first operational aircraft fully to exploit stealth technology.

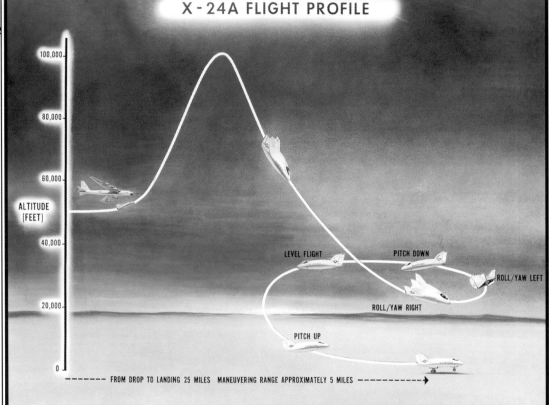

again the XLR 11 and, as with M2, launching had taken place from a B-52. After these flights, the large motor was replaced by three 500-pound (227-kg) thrust Bell hydrogen-peroxide rockets which could be started individually and thus gave the opportunity of providing three levels of thrust. In this guise, the HL-10 conducted tests to determine whether a future space shuttle would need auxiliary power to assist the landing approach.

Following independent research by Martin Marietta from 1959 into lifting-body vehicles, the USAF contracted the company to build four examples of a 4-foot (1.2-m) wingspan and 6-foot 8-inch (2.03-m) length hypersonic unmanned manoeuvrable re-entry vehicle as SV-5Ds, becoming X-23As, and a single larger piloted SV-5P (later becoming X-24A) for low-speed tests. Only three of the X-23As were actually launched, blasted one at a time into space on top of Atlas ballistic missiles, the first launch being on 21 December 1966. A speed of over 16,500 miles per hour (26,550 km/h) and altitude of 500,000 feet (152,400 m) were recorded during the three flight trials, which included ablative shielding tests (heat shield) and re-entry manoeuvring.

The piloted X-24A was similar in many general respects to the Northrop vehicles but used an XLR 11 plus two Bell rocket motors. The first of nine gliding flights took place on 17 April 1969, followed by nineteen powered tests during 1970-71, including a flight in March 1971 of Mach 1.6. After testing was completed, the X-24A was first put into store and then returned to Martin Marietta for reconstruction into the extensively reconfigured X-24B. Thirty-six gliding and powered flights were made with

TOP
X-24A, M2-F3 and HL-10 lifting-body vehicles. (NASA).

ABOVE
Flight profile of the X-24A.

OPPOSITE
Space Shuttle mission STS-7 in June 1983 using the Orbiter Challenger, *and carrying among the crew the first US space woman.*

LEFT,
ABOVE
*X-24B under the wing of the B-52
'motherplane'.*

LEFT,
BELOW
*Avro VZ-9V Avrocar. Steps on the left led to
one of the two cockpits.*
Philip Jarrett collection.

BELOW
*Lockheed Martin concept for a reusable
aeroballistic lifting-body rocket.*
Lockheed Martin/Eric Watanabe.

the X-24B between 1 August 1973 and 26 November 1975, recording a maximum speed of Mach 1.76.

Today, the development of wingless lifting-body vehicles continues, as the photograph below shows. This depicts a Lockheed Martin concept for a reusable aeroballistic rocket with a linear aerospike engine fuelled by over a million pounds of liquid oxygen and liquid hydrogen, enabling it to carry a 40,000-pound (18,145-kg) civil or military payload into low Earth orbit at low cost. Though usually unpiloted, it is expected that such a craft would still make a conventional unpowered landing.

Other wingless or virtually wing-free aircraft have appeared through the decades, of which three deserve special mention. On 5 December 1959 Avro Canada flew the Avrocar on its first tethered test. This,

developed for the US Department of Defense and military designated VZ-9V, was a 'flying saucer' configured vertical take-off and landing vehicle, carrying a crew of two. Three Continental J69 turbojet engines were used to power a central fan to supply a peripheral air curtain and a ground air cushion, while the aerodynamic airframe was to provide lift during horizontal flight. The concept was extensively tested but later abandoned.

In the USA in 1962, Piasecki flight tested two examples of its VZ-8 Aerial Geep, anticipated in production form to provide the US Army with a vehicle that could be driven on land to extend range (via powered wheels), take-off vertically and then be used for airborne observation, liaison and other roles. Although conceived to fly at low level during missions, it was fully capable of

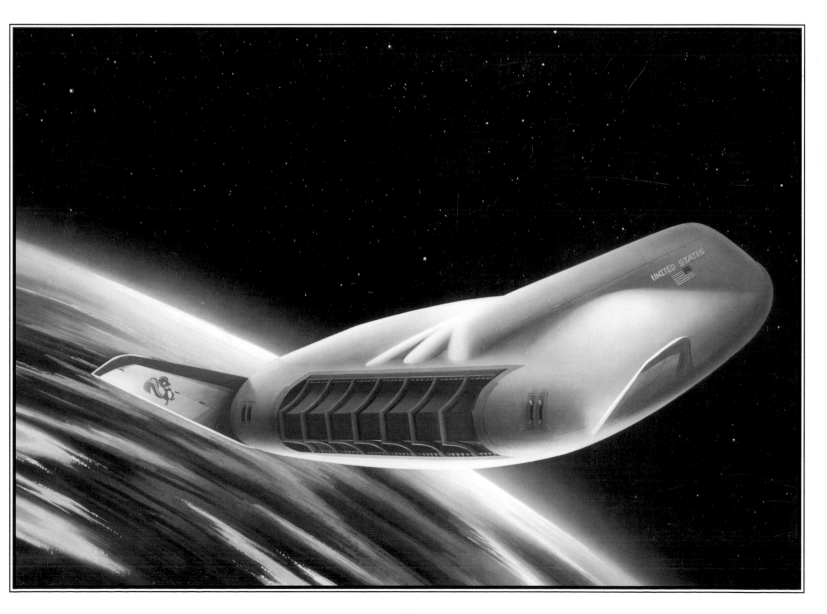

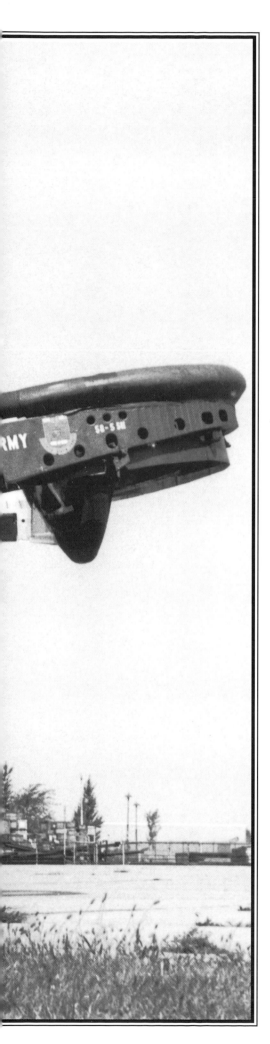

attaining high altitudes. Power came from two 530 shaft hp Turbomeca Artouste turboshaft engines, driving two three-blade ducted rotors that turned in opposite directions.

Coming right up to date, Moller International in the USA has conceived various fan-lift aircraft, of which the four-seat M400 Skycar for commercial marketing is currently under test. Powered by eight highly efficient 160 hp Moller MR 530 rotary piston engines mounted in pairs in the four pods (each engine driving a seven-blade fan), vertical flight is achieved by using sets of computer-reconfigured variable lift vanes at the rear of each pod to redirect thrust. Again, the airframe is expected to generate some of the total lift during forward flight.

The combination of fuselage-generated lift and vertical take-off capability found in the Avrocar and Skycar is a fitting place to end a section on 'wingless' aircraft and begin an overview of other 'unusually configured' vertical take-off and landing aeroplanes. VTOL became a preoccupation of designers in many countries post-war, certain of the advantages over helicopters in particular circumstances and for a wide variety of military and commercial roles.

ABOVE
Moller International M400 Skycar before the engines were installed.

OPPOSITE
Piasecki VZ-8 Aerial Geep.

Chapter Five
Triumph of Ingenuity

The end of the Second World War heralded a peace tainted by ideological divisions in Europe that caused the creation of new and larger power blocs, with Stalin's Soviet Union having significant control over the affairs of Eastern Europe behind an invisible political barrier Winston Churchill called the 'iron curtain'. Because the fight against Germany and Japan had left the victorious nations with immense destructive capability, a mass abandonment of weapons was ruled inappropriate, at least until such time as the 'curtain' could be removed and tensions between East and West relaxed.

Moreover, the war had seen the first operational deployment of jet-powered fighters and bombers, rocketplanes, ballistic and tactical missiles, helicopters, the atomic bomb and other technologies, all in relatively tiny numbers but which rendered the great bulk of currently used equipment virtually outdated, requiring post-war planners to find the budgets necessary to fully modernize their forces. Captured German documents and the willing or enforced emigration of some top German scientists also meant that both East and West had plenty of work to research and benefit from in a race to harness new technologies, with such an awesome arsenal of weapons eventually joining both blocs that peace between the superpowers was guaranteed through assured mutual

destruction if it wasn't, though the war of words and small regional conflicts flared regularly. And it was not just the military that benefited, as new concepts were soon applied to civil aviation as well.

The Sound Barrier

During the war, the pilots of some of the fastest piston-engined fighters with conventional thick wings had experienced severe buffeting during high-speed dives, a force that could literally pull the airframe apart if unchecked. Britain's Hawker Tornado and Typhoon, and America's Republic P-47 Thunderbolt and Lockheed P-38 Lightning were among well-documented cases. This effect was caused by the air flow becoming transonic over the thick wings, and late wartime aircraft such as the German Messerschmitt Me 262 were given thin swept wings as a means of delaying the effect. With the promise of even faster aircraft coming up, it became essential to understand the problem fully and to find more solutions.

In Britain, Miles had begun work on a supersonic research aircraft as early as 1943, under an official specification, to be known as the M-52. Though few fully appreciated the significance at the time, it was to be powered by a turbojet engine with afterburner (rather than rocket power) and was expected to attain 1,000 miles per hour (1,609 km/h) in a dive at 36,000 feet (10,975 m). Its wings were thin and straight, and

ABOVE
Bell XS-1/X-1 46-062 Glamorous Glennis, with Chuck Yeager at the controls in the cramped cockpit.

LEFT
The first Bell XS-1/X-1 46-062, used for the world's first supersonic flight.

PAGE 84-5, LEFT
Douglas X-3 Stilleto, the basic configurational concept of which influenced the design of the Lockheed F-104 Starfighter.

PAGE 85, TOP
The first North American XB-70A Valkyrie, with wingtips drooped.

PAGE 85, BELOW
North American X-15, the fastest aeroplane ever flown, seen here in X-15A-2 modified form with external tanks.

construction was well advanced when the project was cancelled in 1946 because of spending cutbacks and the mistaken assumption that it should have been built with swept wings for supersonic flight.

Similar work had been initiated in the USA from late 1943, and in March 1945 Bell Aircraft received a contract to construct three research aircraft under the official designation of XS-1 (later becoming just X-1), supported by NACA, the USAF and Bell itself. As with the DFS 346 detailed later, the XS-1 had a bullet-shaped fuselage, though married to straight wings of just 3.5 inches (9 cm) thickness, and the airframe was stressed to a massive 18g. The first of the three undertook a gliding flight on 25 January 1946 and a powered test on its fifteenth flight on 9 December that year. Then, during the fiftieth flight of the programme (after being released from under a B-29), this first aircraft attained Mach 1.06

at 42,000 feet (12,800 m), so recording the world's first recognized supersonic flight. Straight wings had proved adequate for the task, just as Miles had predicted, though the XS-1 used the less practical XLR 11 rocket motor for power. The X-1s made a total of 157 flights up to October 1951, reaching Mach 1.45. A second generation of X-1s (also with straight wings) followed from 1951, flying until 1958 and attaining Mach 2.435 on 12 December 1953, again with Charles 'Chuck' Yeager at the controls.

Meanwhile, Douglas had flown the X-3 Stilleto (first flight on 20 October 1952), intended to reach Mach 3. It had been built to investigate the efficiency of turbojets and short 'double wedge' wings, plus provide data on thermodynamic heating at high altitude and high speed, but the maximum level speed attained over twenty flights was Mach 0.95. In the event, it was the sweptwing Bell X-2 that first reached Mach

3, on 27 September 1956 (actually Mach 3.196), although the flight ended in tragedy.

Truly high speeds came with the North American X-15 programme, which involved three single-seat and rocket-powered (initially two XLR 11s and then a 57,000-pound (25,855-kg) thrust XLR 99) aircraft to investigate control, stability and heating during space and atmospheric flight, and in consequence at extreme speeds and extreme altitude. Indeed, the X-15s after air-launching from a B-52 flew high enough for the pilots to be termed astronauts! One hundred and ninety-nine flights were undertaken during the course of the programme, between 8 June 1959 (unpowered) and 24 October 1968, recording an incredible Mach 6.72 on 3 October 1967, while 354,200 feet (107,960 m) altitude was reached on 22 August 1963.

With such a demonstrable ability to build aircraft capable of flying several times

the speed of sound, North American's
selection to construct a new strategic
bomber for the USAF to replace the B-52,
capable of flying the entire mission at an
astonishing Mach 3, appeared a wise choice.
Unfortunately for the company, by 1963
changes in strategic planning and defence
cutbacks meant that the XB-70A Valkyrie
was no longer required as a bomber and so
only two prototypes were sanctioned, for
use as aerodynamic test aircraft. The huge
delta wings with hydraulically-drooping
wingtips and twelve trailing-edge elevons
for control were 105 feet (32 m) in span,
while overall length was 196 feet (59.7 m).
Power came from six 31,000-pound (14,060-
kg) thrust General Electric YJ93-GE-3
turbojets. First flown on 21 September 1964,
the first Valkyrie achieved Mach 3 on 14
October 1965. The second aircraft was lost
in the following year when it collided with
a chase plane. The surviving Valkyrie

subsequently undertook supersonic transport research work with NASA, ending in 1969.

Post-war supersonic development in the Soviet Union began at Podberezye in October 1946, where German engineers assisted in continuing wartime work on the German sweptwing DFS 346, leading to both glider and rocket-powered (two 4,400-pound/2,000-kg thrust Walter 109-509s) aircraft flights after release from an interned B-29 and similar Soviet Tu-4 bombers. It is believed that a DFS 346 attained 683 miles per hour (1,100 km/h) in May 1947, although there remains doubt whether the necessary altitude was sustained to make this a supersonic flight.

Every Which Way – with Helicopters
It comes as a surprise to some to realize that jet aeroplanes and helicopters became

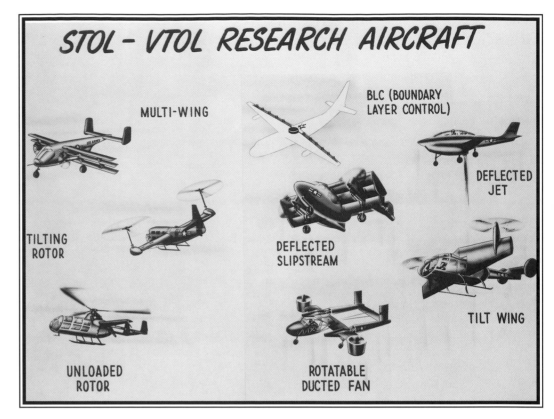

RIGHT
Strangely configured to our modern
thinking was the Piasecki HRP-1 'Flying
Banana', actually a highly successful
helicopter seen here during a mass rescue
demonstration.

BELOW
Lockheed AH-56A Cheyenne, designed as
an advanced attack helicopter and featuring
a pusher propeller.

OPPOSITE, ABOVE
Artist's impression of some of the methods
of short take-off and vertical take-off
research in the 1950s and 1960s, as applied
to actual experimental aircraft.

OPPOSITE, BELOW
Hughes XH-17 pressure-jet helicopter.

HRP-1, nicknamed 'Flying Banana'.

Stranger still was the Hughes XH-17, an experimental pressure-jet helicopter produced under USAF sponsorship and configured for heavy-lift work. First flown on 23 October 1952, it had the largest rotor ever fitted to an engine-powered helicopter, at 130 feet (39.6 m). Two General Electric GE 5500 turbojet engines supplied gas pressure through hollow ducts to exhaust from the rotor tips, thereby turning the huge rotor without the need for a conventional transmission drive system.

In 1956 the Piasecki Helicopter Corporation was renamed Vertol, operating under different management. The previous year, Frank Piasecki had founded Piasecki Aircraft Corporation, and today this company's work includes development of a vectored thrust combat agility demonstrator

operational in the Second World War; they are far more readily associated with post-war flying. Nevertheless, small numbers of single (main) rotor Sikorsky R-4 helicopters joined the US forces from 1944, as the first helicopters actually designed and produced in series for military service, while Germany had struggled against Allied bombing to get

a handfall of its twin-rotor Focke-Achgelis Fa 266 Hornisse transports into operational service, although this helicopter had begun life as a commercial design. The first fully successful tandem rotor helicopter to enter production was the Piasecki PV-3, first flown in March 1945 and joining the US Navy and US Marine Corps from 1947 as the

(VTCAD) under US Army contract, intended to evaluate the benefits in acceleration/deceleration and agility of a vectored-thrust ducted pusher propeller mounted at the rear of an Apache or SuperCobra attack helicopter fuselage. Interestingly, an attack helicopter with a rear-mounted pusher propeller had nearly

ABOVE
Breguet 940 Integral with double-slotted
flaps lowered.

RIGHT
Dornier Do 29 with engines and propellers
deflected downward.

OPPOSITE, ABOVE
Fairey Rotodyne, a successful convertiplane
although its pressure jets were in need of
noise suppression.

OPPOSITE, BELOW
Fairchild VZ-5FA making a tethered vertical
flight.

gone into full-scale production some thirty
years before, as the Lockheed AH-56A
Cheyenne, when 375 were ordered for the
US Army in 1968 but cancelled the
following year. The Cheyenne used its 3,435
shaft hp General Electric T64-GE-16
turboshaft engine to drive the main rotor,
anti-torque tail rotor and pusher propeller,

and attained 253 miles per hour (407 km/h).

Every Which Way – with Aeroplanes
It had long been recognized that an aircraft
combining the best attributes of a helicopter
and a transport aeroplane would be
extremely useful to both military and
commercial operations, but the many
attempts to produce such a machine have

up to recently ended after flight-testing of demonstrators. That is not to say they were unsuccessful. Far from it. A number of these 'convertiplanes' were of sufficient maturity to have warranted production had the funds been made available, if that was the original aim rather than just pure research.

In the most simplistic terms, a helicopter has the disadvantages of short range and modest speed, while a conventional fixed-wing aeroplane cannot take-off and land vertically or hover. If, however, a means could be found for a transport aeroplane to lift vertically and then gain sufficient forward speed for the large wings to produce most or all of the required lift for horizontal flight, then high speeds and longer range could be guaranteed.

The world's first large vertical take-off and landing (VTOL) transport was the British Fairey Rotodyne, which was first

ABOVE

Dornier Do 31E3 second demonstrator in vertical flight, with lift jet doors open.

OPPOSITE,

ABOVE

Rolls-Royce Thrust-Measuring Rig, nicknamed 'Flying Bedstead', first flown in August 1954 to help in the development of VTOL aircraft. The jetpipes of the two Nene engines were downward turned by ninety degrees to give vertical thrust.

BELOW

Dornier's second hovering test rig for Do 31 development, the 'Big Rig'.

flown on 6 November 1957. This, in Rotodyne Y prototype form, had a transport-type fuselage accommodating a crew of two and forty passengers, fixed wings of 46 feet 6 inches (14.17 m) span carrying two 3,000 shaft hp Napier Eland NEL3 turboprop engines, and a rotor of 90 feet (27.4 m) diameter with tip-mounted pressure jets. In addition to driving the main propellers, the engines were coupled to compressors that produced air for the rotor pressure jets (at which fuel was mixed to create thrust to turn the rotor).

Although capable of operating as a pure helicopter, the Rotodyne was expected to use its rotor (while under power) for vertical flight and to gain initial horizontal speed, after which it would autorotate to contribute some lift to the main lift and forward thrust then generated by the wings and propellers. The first transition from vertical to horizontal flight was on 10 April 1958.

Though there was great commercial interest in production examples, the British Government ended the programme in 1962.

Deflected slipstream proved to be another perfectly sound method of achieving short take-off or vertical flight, though when applied to the US Army-sponsored VZ-5FA built by Fairchild in the 1950s it produced a rather peculiar outcome. With a 1,024 shaft hp General Electric YT58-GE-2 turboshaft engine installed in the fuselage to drive four propellers, it used large wing flaps that extended downward to deflect the propeller slipstream towards the ground for vertical take off, aided by the aircraft resting on its tailskid and with the nose pointing up at an angle of some forty-five degrees. The single VZ-5FA made its first tethered flight on 18 November 1959.

STOL (not VTOL) performance using the deflected slipstream technique was

achieved highly successfully by the French Breguet 940 Integral, which first flew on 21 May 1958. The slipstream from the four Turbomeca Turmo turboshafts with three-blade propellers was blown over the whole of the wings and large double-slotted flaps. Four examples of the pre-production 941S derivative joined the French Armée de l'Air in the latter 1960s. (See page 89)

In Germany, Dornier built the Do 29 to research into the deflected propeller technique for achieving very short take-off and possibly vertical take-off flight, with each of the two 270 hp Lycoming GO-480-B1A6 piston engines and propellers able to pivot downward by up to ninety degrees. Trials with the Do 29 began in late 1958.

Rolls-Royce in Britain, Dornier in Germany and others found that constructing open-structure hovering test rigs was a useful first step in

understanding the problems associated with the flight, stability and control of jet-powered vertical take-off aircraft. Dornier, having flown a totally open rig, produced a second hovering rig that formed a mid-stage in the development of its Do 31E experimental VTOL transport aircraft.

The Do 31E itself had accommodation for the crew plus thirty-four troops, twenty-four stretchers or cargo in a typical transport aircraft fuselage, and was seen as useful not only in general transport terms but for supporting VTOL combat aircraft in the field. The wings carried two 15,500-pound (7,030-kg) thrust Rolls-Royce Pegasus 5-2 vectored engines, while at each wingtip was attached a removable pod with four 4,400-pound (1,995-kg) thrust RB 162-4D lift jets. Two flying Do 31Es were constructed, recording the first take-off on 10 February 1967 and the first transition

ABOVE
EWR VJ 101C X1 in horizontal flight, with wingtip pods fully fore-and-aft.

OPPOSITE
Vertol Model 76, military designated VZ-2A, a US Army- and Navy-sponsored small and inexpensive tilt-wing research aircraft that first flew on 13 August 1957, intended to test this new technology prior to trials with larger aircraft .

from vertical to horizontal flight on 16 December that year. Hundreds of test flights were made until 1970, but the projected military and civil production derivatives never materialized.

Tilting Trials

Still in Germany, EWR developed the VJ 101C as a single-seat experimental VTOL aircraft, intended to provide data for the design of a Mach 2 VTOL fighter for operational service. Two VJ 101Cs were built, the first having two 2,750-pound (1,247-kg) thrust Rolls-Royce RB 145 turbojets in each of two swivelling wingtip pods and two more vertically mounted in the fuselage to perform only as lift jets and used in VTOL or transitional flight (six engines in total). The second aircraft had afterburning engines in the wingtip pods. VJ 101C X1 made its first free hovering flight on 10 April 1963, its first conventional take-off on 31 August, and first transition on 20 September. In transition from horizontal to vertical flight, the wingtip pods remained horizontal until speed reduced to 190 miles per hour (305 km/h), when they were tilted forty-five degrees, with full ninety-degree tilt when airspeed was below 57 miles per hour (92 km/h), allowing the aircraft to slow towards hover. In the event, no production developments followed, although the unaugmented X1 demonstrated supersonic speed (Mach 1.08).

The prospect of a V/STOL convertiplane transport for military service was so appealing during the 1950s and '60s that many research aircraft were built and flown to prove and develop the technologies, mostly relying on propellers that tilted in one form or another. In the event, no such aircraft has yet entered full military or commercial service, although the present-day Osprey seems likely to break new ground and actually join the US forces.

The Fairchild X-18 of 1959, LTV/Hiller/Ryan XC-142A of 1964 and Canadair CL-84 of 1965 first appearances were VTOL transport types that adopted tilting wing technology (the propellers tilting with the wings). All followed the little Boeing Vertol VZ-2A research aircraft of 1957 into the air. The X-18's sole role was research and was never intended to be

developed for production. It was based on a converted Chase YC-122 transport aircraft, fitted with two Allison T40 turboprop engines and Curtiss-Wright contra-rotating propellers taken from the US Navy's abandoned tail-sitting fighter programmes (see Convair XFY-1 and Lockheed XFV-1, page 101). First flown on 24 November 1959 after a conventional take-off, the X-18's most important contribution was to help in the development of the later XC-142A.

The XC-142A itself was jointly developed by three US manufacturers under USAF programme management and was expected eventually to lead to production aircraft entering service with the US forces, to be capable of transporting troops or supplies from land bases or assault ships to unprepared forward positions in any weather. The wing, which carried four 2,850 shaft hp turboprop engines, could tilt through one hundred degrees to provide the necessary vertical/horizontal flight control. Accommodation was very similar to that of the Do 31. Five flying prototypes were built, with flight tests starting on 29 September 1964 in conventional form. Hovering was first accomplished on 29 December and a transition completed on 11 January 1965. Trials were highly successful and the future for the aircraft appeared bright. In May 1966 evaluation from the aircraft carrier USS *Bennington* proved that it could be operated from ships underway. By then the USAF had requested details on a production version, but like so many other advanced programmes of the time, funding was not forthcoming.

One of the smallest tilt-wing aircraft intended to spawn eventual production was the Canadian Canadair CL-84, to be an armed close support and utility transport in developed form, able to carry sixteen troops. Two 1,400 shaft hp Lycoming T53 turboshaft engines were mounted on the wing of the prototype, which could tilt one hundred degrees, and a speed of over 320 miles per hour (515 km/h) was anticipated. First hovered on 7 May 1965, the single prototype totalled 405 flying hours in 305

flights (including military evaluation) before an accident ended its career. Three improved examples followed as CL-84-1s (first flown in 1970), and other models were anticipated, but, again, full production of this worthy aircraft did not take place.

Instead of tilting wings, Bell built its X-22A as a tilting-duct research aircraft for use in a US tri-service project under the overall management and contract of the Navy. Four 1,250 shaft hp General Electric YT58-GE-8D turboshaft engines carried ahead of the rear-mounted wings drove three-blade propellers mounted in ducts on the wingtips and front fuselage, each of the four ducts being capable of tilting through ninety-five degrees (at a turn rate of five degrees per second) according to the flight mode, and each having an elevon control surface in the slipstream. First flown on 17 March 1966, the two prototypes made hundreds of flights in vertical, short take-off, horizontal and transitional modes up to 1984.

Meanwhile, on 23 August 1955 the first flight of the four-seat Bell XV-3 had taken place. This was an experimental convertiplane with a single 450 hp Pratt & Whitney R-985 piston engine driving two 33-foot (10-m) tiltable proprotors at the tips of the wings (about 31-foot/9.4-m span). The proprotors were to act as both helicopter rotors and aeroplane propellers, depending upon whether they were in horizontal position for vertical flight or tilted down to vertical position for high-speed horizontal flight, with the full tilt taking only ten–fifteen seconds. Of course, because of the diameter of the proprotors, landing could not be effected without the blades tilted to horizontal or near horizontal helicopter mode. Maximum level speed was 181 miles per hour (291 km/h). Two XV-3s

Canadair CL-84-1s with wings tilted. Note the tailplanes, which tilted with the wings except when in vertical flight.

were built, and these amassed over 250 flights as the world's first fixed-wing aircraft to demonstrate full rotor tilting.

Two decades later Bell resurrected the concept for its very differently configured XV-15, first flown on 3 May 1977 and used to assess the operational flight envelope and potential military/commercial applications for such an aircraft.

Then, in 1989, proprotor technology reappeared in potentially its most useful form, as a joint effort by Bell and Boeing and known as the V-22 Osprey, which made its maiden flight on 19 March. As a twin turboshaft tilt-rotor type of larger size than the XV-15, it is the first such aircraft

expected to achieve mass production, and is scheduled for initial operational capability with the US military forces from the year 2001. Various roles are planned, including troop and cargo transportation, assault, medical evacuation, combat search and rescue, and special operations. The proprotors are each 38 feet (11.6 m) in diameter, driven by two 6,150 shaft hp Allison T406-AD-400 turboshaft engines. Finally revealing the full potential of convertiplanes, Osprey can take-off and land as a helicopter, yet attain 361 miles per hour (581 km/h) in aeroplane flight mode, and still carry a 20,000-pound (9,072-kg) load for well over 2,000 miles (3,218 km).

ABOVE
Bell XV-3 with proprotors in vertical aeroplane mode.

OPPOSITE
Bell X-22A in hovering flight, benefiting from ground effect.

What goes up

It is common knowledge that Hawker Siddeley in Britain developed the world's first operational fixed-wing V/STOL combat aircraft as the original Harrier, which joined the RAF in 1969. The general aircraft type remains in production today by British Aerospace and McDonnell Douglas, though in much improved forms for land and sea operations. In the Soviet Union, Yakovlev developed the first-generation Yak-36 (now out of service) and then the Yak-141 second-generation VTOL combat aircraft, both differing from the earlier Harrier by having separate downward-angled lift-jets to assist vertical flying in addition to the main horizontally-installed turbofan with vectored thrust used during all aspects of flight.

Combining vertical flight with high-speed combat aircraft was a challenge that had occupied designers since the 1940s. Of course, Bachem in wartime Germany had developed a vertically-launched interceptor as the Natter (see text and photograph, pages 56-7), but this rocketplane concept was hardly worth pursuing postwar. A contemporary concept was the Focke-Wulf Triebflügel, a tail-sitting thrust-wing fighter with three wings that rotated around the fuselage, driven by a ramjet at each tip. Although this remained a 'paper' project, it is interesting to note that a speed of 621 miles per hour (1,000 km/h) was projected, combined with long endurance. But, clearly, relying on rotors would not be the longer-term answer.

The prospect of a vertical take-off fighter able to operate from a small platform instead of a huge carrier deck had appeal to the US Navy and in 1950 it held a design competition to encourage proposals,

Bell-Boeing V-22 Osprey, the complete propulsion assembly able to tilt through 97.5 degrees. Maximum troop accommodation is twenty-four.

resulting in both Convair and Lockheed receiving contracts to build two prototypes each as XFY-1 Pogo and XFV-1 Salmon (sometimes called Vertical Riser) respectively. As with the Focke-Wulf design, these were tail-sitters, using castor-wheels on legs attached to the trailing-edge of the cruciform wings and/or tail fins as undercarriage units. Each type was powered by a 5,850 equivalent shaft hp Allison YT40 turboprop engine driving Curtiss-Wright Turboelectric co-axial contra-rotating propellers; the turboprop was itself a very new form of engine still in its infancy. Each pilot sat on a 'gimbal' seat able to tilt according to the flight mode, and gun or rocket armament was carried in wingtip pods.

Following a large number of tethered flights using a special test rig constructed in a naval airship hangar at Moffett Field, free flying commenced. The first to fly was the Lockheed Salmon, in March 1954, but this was only ever flown horizontally using a special undercarriage rig and only one prototype was completed before the Navy terminated development. Convair's Pogo first flew on 2 August 1954 in vertical flight and completed a further seventy vertical take-offs and landings before attempting a transition to and from horizontal flight on 2 November that same year. But, despite its demonstrated ability to fly in all modes and its possessing a speed of around 500 miles per hour (805 km/h), stability problems and other factors led to the Pogo also being abandoned by the Navy.

Meanwhile, the US Navy and USAF had turned to Ryan to develop an experimental pure-jet VTOL aircraft, ordering two examples as delta-winged X-13 Vertijets. These represented the culmination of work by Ryan (on its Model 38) that dated from a Navy feasibility study contract of 1947. However, the Model 38 itself owed something to Ryan's early work with jet-boosted fighters that had began in 1943, when the company had received a contract from the US Navy to construct prototypes of its piston-engined Model 28 that also

incorporated a turbojet booster engine in the tail as a 'mixed' power fighter. Production examples, as FR-1 Fireballs, had joined the US Navy for a brief period of service between March 1945 and 1947. Meanwhile, in November 1946 Ryan had flown its XF2R-1, an experimental fighter with a turboprop engine in the nose and turbojet in the tail. As even the piston/turbojet Fireball, from which the XF2R-1 had been developed, had shown the possibility of a thrust-to-weight ratio better than 1 to 1, Ryan had been encouraged to extend its research on jet aircraft.

ABOVE
Convair XFY-1 Pogo in vertical flight.

OPPOSITE
Lockheed XFV-1 Salmon tail-sitting fighter from the US Naval Aviation Museum.
Austin J. Brown.

Each Vertijet was powered by a 10,000-pound (4,535-kg) thrust Rolls-Royce Avon turbojet, and the first flew on 10 December 1955 in conventional horizontal flight mode using a temporary undercarriage rig. The first brief vertical hovering flight was recorded on 28 May 1956 and then on 28 November the first-ever transition from horizontal to vertical flight and back by a jet aircraft was made at 6,000 feet (1,830 m). Even more impressive was the mission of 11 April 1957, when an X-13 took-off vertically, made a transition to horizontal flight and undertook various manoeuvres before returning to Edwards base for a vertical landing. As a whole, the X-13 programme was a complete success, proving beyond doubt that jet VTOL aircraft were both possible and practical.

A contemporary of the X-13 was the

Short Brothers SC.1, the first fixed-wing VTOL aircraft to fly in the United Kingdom. It possessed fewer of the advanced aerodynamicsto be found on the Vertijet, as it had been developed to an official specification purely for research, without any pseudo-combat aircraft aspirations, although it too had delta wings. Construction of the SC.1 began in 1954 and the first of two aircraft made its maiden flight on 2 April 1957 from Boscombe Down, although then as a conventional aeroplane in horizontal flight. The second SC.1 was the first to enter a series of tethered vertical flight trials, starting on 23 May 1958, with untethered vertical take-offs from 25 October, and the all-important first transition from vertical to horizontal flight and back again on 6 April 1960. Not to be left out of the headlines, the original SC.1

recorded the first-ever crossing of the English Channel by a jet-lift aircraft some thirteen months later.

Unlike the X-13, the SC.1 had been designed from the outset to land on a conventional undercarriage, with the fuselage in a horizontal attitude. Power came from five 2,130-pound (966-kg) thrust Rolls-Royce RB.108 turbojets, four installed vertically in the mid-fuselage to provide jet-lift but also able to be inclined slightly forwards and backwards to assist in braking and forward thrust, while the fifth was mounted horizontally for forward thrust only. Control nozzles for stability at the wingtips, tail and nose used high-pressure air bled from engine compressors. As time would tell, this engine arrangement was never adopted for a British production aircraft, with the Harriers relying instead on a single engine with vectoring nozzles, but a variation on the theme was used in the Soviet Yakovlevs mentioned earlier, resulting from independent research.

Perhaps the strangest of all the experimental VTOL 'aircraft' to fly were the French SNECMA C.450-01 Coléoptère and the Bell Rocket and Jet Belts. The Coléoptère was a tail-sitting research

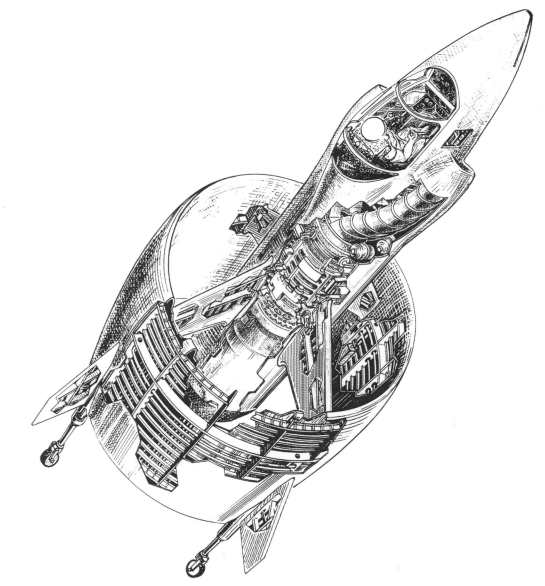

aircraft, powered by an 8,160-pound (3,700-kg) thrust SNECMA Atar 101EV turbojet installed in the rear fuselage, surrounded by an annular wing with four fins and rudders for directional control. It followed earlier Atar Volant unmanned and then piloted rigs used for vertical flight trials, and differed principally in having the capability to perform full transitions. The first untethered vertical flight was recorded on 6 May 1959, but the aircraft was lost in an accident on 25 July during a transition flight, when it went out of control. Fortunately, the pilot was able to use his ejection seat to escape. The aircraft had, however, proven the general concept.

Bell's highly successful and unique Rocket and Jet Belts resulted from an original idea said to have been first drawn out in the desert sand near Edwards Air

Command to develop the SRLD into a
working system. For this, Aerojet-General
developed a 280-pound (127-kg) variable
thrust rocket motor. Thrust control was
effected by the pilot's right-hand squeeze
throttle, while jetavator gas deflectors
provided yaw control via the pilot's left-
hand controls. Following a large number of
tethered trials, on 20 April 1961 Harold
Graham made the first-ever free flight with
the SRLD, lasting thirteen seconds and
flying slowly forward at minimal height. As
the operating envelope was extended, soon
the SRLD was demonstrating flights of 860
feet (262 m) length, altitudes of 60 feet (18
m) and speeds of almost 60 miles per hour
(96 km/h), ideal for infantry to cross
minefields, rivers, defences and other
obstacles or for amphibious landings.
Hundreds of flights were made with the
SRLD, including a special demonstration to
President Kennedy in October 1961, when a
pilot lifted from an amphibious craft and
flew over water before landing directly in
front of the President.

One shortcoming of the Rocket Belt was
the limited duration of the rocket motor.
Such was the potential of the system,
however, that the US Army contracted Bell
to develop a Jet Belt, which used a Williams
Research Corporation WR-19 turbojet engine
in place of the rocket motor. With this, an
endurance of up to 26 minutes was
anticipated. First flown on 7 April 1969,

ABOVE
Bell Aerosystems Jet Belt

ABOVE RIGHT
*Artist's drawing of a Hiller VZ-1 Do-Nut
one-man infantry VTOL flying platform of
1959, of which two were built for
experimental trials with the US Army. It
used a ducted propeller to provide thrust.*

OPPOSITE
*Saunders-Roe SR.A/1 jet flying-boat fighter
TG263, the first and only prototype to
survive the test programme.*

Force Base by Bell Aerosystems' engineer
Wendell Moore, in 1953. The initial Small
Rocket Lift Device (SRLD) or Rocket Belt
was a minimum strap-on back-pack system
intended to lift a man in controlled flight
over a short distance. For early trials, an
experimental unit was devised using
nitrogen gas and two downward facing
nozzles, initially tested on a rig to evaluate
stability and other technical issues. It
quickly became clear that the nozzles were
too close to the pilot, as one operator lost
his jacket sleeves in the blast.

US Army interest was inevitable and in
1960 Bell received a contract from the
Transportation, Research and Engineering

many successful flights were made, but neither this nor the Rocket system went into production. Interestingly, Bell and Williams went on to develop two-person flying platforms that were so stable the crew only had to lean in the direction they wanted to fly, thereby requiring just thrust control. Among the expected applications was astronaut mobility on the Moon.

No runway required

The vulnerability of airfields to enemy attack had been well demonstrated in the early years of the Second World War, most completely during the Luftwaffe's opening onslaught on the Soviet Union on 22 June 1941, when 1,811 Soviet aircraft were destroyed before nightfall, 1,489 on the ground. To remove that vulnerability, two possible solutions were obvious, to adopt vertical take-off aircraft or base aircraft on water. In Britain, VTOL was not a priority

for development at that time, but in 1943 Saunders-Roe proposed a single-seat jet flying-boat fighter which could not be put out of action by the destruction of land airfields and also had the advantage of needing no prepared bases when operated away from home. By 1944 the company had received an official specification and contract for development.

The principal feature of the SR.A/1, as it became known, was its single-step hull housing two 3,250–3,850-pound (1,474–1,746-kg) thrust Metropolitan-Vickers Beryl MVBI turbojets in its sides, with an air intake in the nose. Armament was four 20-mm cannon. The first of three aircraft was flown on 16 July 1947, and the SR.A/1 became the first flying-boat ever to exceed 500 miles per hour(805 km/h). The need to find new engines for any further production aircraft and other issues held

back the programme until, despite an inverted fly-past at the 1948 Farnborough Air Show, it was decided that the large hull compromised speed and manoeuvrability compared with the latest land fighters and the programme was terminated.

In the USA, Convair built and tested its own jet flying-boat fighter as the Sea Dart, first taking-off from San Diego Bay on 9 April 1953 and featuring the fruit of the company's pioneering work on delta wings. The original XF2Y-1 prototype had two Westinghouse J34-WE-42 turbojets with a combined thrust of 8,500 pounds (3,855 kg) with afterburning, but the second aircraft (YF2Y-1) used J46s of 6,000-pound (2,722-kg) afterburning thrust each, the intakes on both aircraft located above and behind the wing leading edge to keep them free from water spray. It was the YF2Y-1 that made history by becoming the first seaplane

LEFT
Convair Sea Dart with twin hydroskis deployed.

BELOW
The fourth Soviet KM Kaspian Monster
ekranoplan.
Via Russian Aviation Research Trust.

OPPOSITE, ABOVE
*West Germany was among other nations that
experimented with the surface-effect concept,
using the small RFB X-114.*

OPPOSITE, BELOW
*The amazing Pitts S-2B biplane modified by
airshow aerobatic pilot, Craig Hosking, with a
second undercarriage on the upper wing to
enable him to take-off and land upside down. An
electric winch helps cockpit entry.*
Chris Gingell.

to exceed Mach 1, in a shallow dive on 3 August 1954, having first climbed to 34,000 feet (10,360 m), undertaken as a speed run during a routine test flight sandwiched into a programme of coastal take-offs and landings (but was lost later that year). Eventually, three more Sea Darts joined the programme but, despite outstanding potential, there was to be no production. A clever design innovation was the use of a hydroski or twin skis to avoid the need for a large flying-boat hull, with the aircraft initially floating with its wings only an inch or two above the water but climbing on to its retractable skis almost immediately the taxi run began to lift the airframe out of the water for take-off.

The Soviet Union also conducted its own jet flying-boat experiments, although as far as it is known they were for quite different purposes, many aimed at the eventual goal of producing bombers, anti-submarine aircraft and high-speed/long-range transports. By far the longest and heaviest of all sea-going 'aircraft' the world has ever known was the Soviet KM *Kaspian Monster*, correctly termed a Power-Augmented Ram Wing in Ground Effect Machine (PAR-WIG) or merely

Ekranoplan to the Soviets. This used a surface-effect phenomenon to achieve high speed and long range, whereby if an aeroplane flies at such low level that its altitude is equal to about half its wing span, a dynamic cushion of air is 'captured' between the wings and the surface and so inhibits downwash and dramatically cuts induced drag. Of course, normal flying would be possible when required. The *Kaspian Monster*, as the largest of all such PAR-WIG aircraft and by

far the most incredible, of which eight appeared from 1965, was powered by ten 28,600-pound (13,000-kg) thrust Rybinsk VD-7 turbojets. Of varying proportions, the greatest span and length of any aircraft of the series were about 131 feet (40 m) and 348 feet (106 m) respectively, with weights up to 1,190,500 pounds (540,000 kg). Cruise speed has been quoted at 310 miles per hour (500 km/h) and range 1,865 miles (3,000 km). At least one was seen carrying surface-to-surface missiles, although roles would

Flying Fish

Passenger and freight civil transports have, on the whole, been among the most conventional aircraft, although some early exceptions to this rule have been detailed previously. The workhorses of the Second World War, such as militarized versions of the DC-3 and DC-4, set the pattern for many post-war commercial aircraft and even today most large jets retain the basic attributes. But for military transportation, in particular, the need to drive heavy vehicles straight into the fuselage hold, load and unload bulk items rapidly, or air-drop large cargoes, led to the post-war proliferation of twin-boom designs with easy rear access, although most later gave way to more 'conventional' aircraft with simple upswept 'beaver tail' rear fuselages to provide aft access.

Fairchild in the USA was one of many companies that went through this metamorphosis, adding also an extra dimension with its XC-120 Pack-Plane. Based on its twin-boom C-119 Packet military transport, the Pack-Plane was developed to a USAF contract and first flew on 11 August 1950, featuring a totally detachable lower fuselage section with clam-shell loading doors at both ends, allowing various military loads to be left behind in this 'containerized' form while the aircraft returned for a new lower pack. In tests it proved successful but remained a prototype.

The post-war need to commercially transport 'outsized' cargoes did, however, lead to small numbers of extraordinary civil aircraft, the majority produced as conversions of existing types, their fuselages enlarged as appropriate to the given task. Among the earliest and largest of these were the Guppies, originally devised by Aero Spacelines as conversions of old Boeing Stratocruiser piston airliners or related C-97 military transports to permit the carriage of rocket booster sections or other wide and high loads. The initial version was the B-377PG Pregnant Guppy, which took to the air in 1962. Each Guppy model had a new and huge bulbous lobe structure built over the existing fuselage, with the entire front

have included high-speed reinforcement. But whilst PAR-WIGs seemed to promise the greatest advance in aviation since the jet engine, particularly for rapid long-distance transportation, the concept appears to have fizzled out, although it is possible that some remaining KMs are still operated (at least two were lost, in 1969 and 1980).

Before leaving surface-effect water-borne aircraft, it is interesting to record that in 1963 Bell Aerospace had initiated development of an Air Cushion Landing

System for transport aircraft (then also considered a possible system for the Space Shuttle), permitting touch-down on water, swamp land, snow, and other soft or rough surfaces. Trials began with a modified Lake LA-4 amphibian, progressing on to a large de Havilland Canada DHC-5 Buffalo transport loaned by the Canadian Department of National Defence and redesignated the XC-8A. The first take-off by the XC-8A with the ACLS took place on 31 March 1975.

A fitting end to this book on strange but wonderful aircraft comes with the work of one of the world's most prolific and respected designers, Elbert 'Burt' Rutan. Among the ranks of enthusiast constructors who build their own aircraft for private use, Rutan's rear-winged VariViggen and VariEze two-seat 'homebuilts' are legend, while he also designed the *Voyager* trimaran monoplane in which his brother Richard and Jeana Yeager made history during 14–23 December 1986 by successfully completing the first-ever non-stop and unrefuelled aeroplane flight around the world, in so doing establishing an absolute distance record of 24,986.664 miles (40,212,139 km).

To a NASA requirement, Burt Rutan was responsible for designing the pivoting-wing AD-1 for oblique-wing research and, having set up Scaled Composites Inc, designed several very unusual aircraft with production possibilities. These include the composites-constructed Rutan 151 ARES agile-response effective-support military aircraft with rear-mounted wings, swept-forward canards and a fuselage with an offset 2,950-pound (1,338-kg) thrust Pratt & Whitney JT15D-1 turbofan, intended as an inexpensive battlefield attack aircraft. His Predator 480 was built as an agricultural

end of the fuselage hinging to one side to allow straight-in loading. For the Pregnant Guppy, the cabin became 19 feet 9 inches (6.02 m) high, instead of the standard Stratocruiser height of under 9 feet (2.74 m). The Super Guppy was the most-produced variant, offering a hold height of 25 feet 6 inches (7.77 m) and width of 25 feet 1 inch (7.65m). In 1996, Super Guppies were still being used to support the European Airbus airliner programme, transporting large airframe sections between manufacturing

and assembly factories in various countries. Their use by Airbus is, however, coming to an end and a modern replacement first flew on 13 September 1994 as the SATIC A300-600ST Super Transporter, known as Beluga and based on the Airbus A300-600. Beluga provides a freight compartment of nearly 124 feet (37.8m) usable length by over 24 feet (7.3 m) width, and offers a 100,310-pound (45,500 kg) payload. Four have been ordered by Airbus and further production for other operators is possible.

ABOVE LEFT
Fairchild XC-120 Pack-Plane.

LEFT
Super Guppy taking on board an airliner assembly payload.

OPPOSITE, ABOVE
The first of four SATIC A300-600ST Super Transporters for Airbus Industrie, known as Belugas.

MIDDLE
Scaled Composites ARES combat aircraft.

BELOW
Scaled Composites Predator 480 proof-of-concept agricultural aircraft.

aircraft and first flew in 1984, while the ATTT followed in 1987 as a scale tactical transport, both the Predator 480 and ATTT flown as proof-of-concept aircraft. In 1996, work at Scaled on unusual aircraft continues, the asymmetrical 201-11 Boomerang five-seat light aircraft having a passing similarity in configurational concept to the wartime Bv 141.

Of course, Rutan is not alone in designing unusually-configured private aircraft, and among many that have come from the drawing boards of others is a representative of the powered sailplane fraternity, the Swiss Farner HF Colibri 1 SL.

From the large to the small – with wings, power plants and undercarriages in almost every conceivable position – strangely-configured aircraft have played an important role in pushing the boundaries of aviation knowledge and competence to new ranges of excellence. Some succeeded, others did not, but all have contributed to the rich tapestry of flight, past and present, ensuring that life for the aviation-minded never becomes boring.

INDEX